MW00577386

BEST OF

Ljubljana

Fionn Davenport

How to use this book

Colour-Coding & Maps

Each chapter has a colour code along the banner at the top of the page which is also used for text and symbols on maps (eg all venues reviewed in the Highlights chapter are orange on the maps). The fold-out maps inside the front and back covers are numbered from 1 to 5. All sights and venues in the text have map references; eg (4, D5) means Map 4, grid reference D5. See p64 for map symbols.

Prices

Multiple prices listed with reviews (eg 700/500SIT) usually indicate adult/concession admission to a venue. Concession prices can include senior, student, member or coupon discounts. Meal cost and room rate categories are listed at the start of the Eating and Sleeping chapters, respectively.

Text Symbols

☎	telephone
✉	address
🖳	email/website address
€	admission
🕑	opening hours
ⓘ	information
Ⓜ	metro
🚍	bus
Ⓟ	parking available
♿	wheelchair access
✗	on-site/nearby eatery
👶	child-friendly venue
Ⓥ	good vegetarian selection

Best of Ljubljana
1st edition – Jun 2006

Published by Lonely Planet Publications Pty Ltd
ABN 36 005 607 983

Australia Head Office, Locked Bag 1, Footscray, Vic 3011
☎ 03 8379 8000 fax 03 8379 8111
🖳 talk2us@lonelyplanet.com.au
USA 150 Linden St, Oakland, CA 94607
☎ 510 893 8555 toll free 800 275 8555
fax 510 893 8572
🖳 info@lonelyplanet.com
UK 72–82 Rosebery Avenue, London EC1R 4RW
☎ 020 7841 9000 fax 020 7841 9001
🖳 go@lonelyplanet.co.uk

This title was commissioned in Lonely Planet's London office by Fiona Buchan and produced by Cambridge Publishing Management Limited. **Thanks** to Glenn Beanland, David Burnett, Piotr Czajkowski, Brendan Dempsey, Ryan Evans, Fayette Fox, Quentin Frayne, Michala Green, Mark Griffiths, Imogen Hall, Corey Hutchison, Glenn van der Knijff, Marika Kozak, Charles Rawlings-Way, Michael Ruff, Wibowo Rusli, Fiona Siseman, Ray Thomson, Tashi Wheeler, Liz White, Rachel Wood

Photographs by Lonely Planet Images and Jonathan Smith except for the following: p13 Walter Bibikow/age fotostock, p23 Richard I'Anson/Lonely Planet Images, p24 Jon Davison/Lonely Planet Images, p25 Craig Pershouse/Lonely Planet Images.

Cover photograph Richard I'Anson/Lonely Planet Images, Cobbled laneway

All images are copyright of the photographers unless otherwise indicated. Many of the images in this guide are available for licensing from Lonely Planet Images: www.lonelyplanetimages.com.

ISBN 1 74104 824 9

Printed through Colorcraft Ltd, Hong Kong.
Printed in China

Contents

From the Publisher

THE AUTHOR
Fionn Davenport

No sooner did Fionn climb aboard a taxi at the airport than he knew this was going to be a great place: the taxi driver was both honest and friendly and the car absolutely spotless. It set the tone for Ljubljana as a whole, which revealed itself to be totally easy-going and relaxed. It is the kind of city that won't bend over to impress you but pulls out all the stops to make you feel welcome. And that's all down to the people – and the *jota*.

Petra Stušek of the Slovene Tourist Board, Branko Dvorščak at Postojna and the Slovene Embassy in Dublin were all extremely helpful in getting my research up and running. Once in Ljubljana, the following were gracious enough to let me into their lives: Maja, Jaka, Uroš, Sabina, Alica, Matevž, Pavle, Romina, Mira, Igor, Pero, Andrej, São, Matej, Saša and the Hočevar family – Meta, Janez, Maja, Miha, Gašper and Matevž. A huge thanks to Damjan Možina for his friendship and, finally, to Jera Ivanc, who not only introduced me to everyone listed above but managed to reveal Ljubljana in all its mysterical glory. *Hvala lepa*. I owe you one.

LONELY PLANET AUTHORS

Why is our travel information the best in the world? It's simple: our authors are independent, dedicated travellers. They don't research using just the Internet or phone, and they don't take freebies in exchange for positive coverage. They travel widely, to all the popular spots and off the beaten track. They personally visit thousands of hotels, restaurants, cafés, bars, galleries, palaces, museums and more – and they take pride in getting all the details right, and telling it how it is. For more, see the authors section on **www.lonelyplanet.com**.

PHOTOGRAPHER
Jonathan Smith

Raised in rural Aberdeenshire, Jon graduated from St Andrews University in 1994 with an MA in German and little idea of what to do with his life. After a spell teaching languages in newly independent Lithuania, he spent three years travelling around the former USSR, trying to carve himself a niche as a freelance travel photographer.

Since then his byline has appeared in over 100 Lonely Planet titles and recent commissions have included Lonely Planet's *Paris*, *St Petersburg* and *Moscow* city guides. Jon says the highlights of his first visit to Ljubljana were sipping *kava s smetano* on Prešernov trg, bargain-hunting at the antiques flea market and watching local basketball heroes Olimpija Ljubljana clash with Lithuania's mighty Žalgiris Kaunas.

SEND US YOUR FEEDBACK

We love to hear from travellers – your comments keep us on our toes and help make our books better. Our well-travelled team reads every word on what you loved or loathed about this book. Although we cannot reply individually to postal submissions, we always guarantee that your feedback goes straight to the appropriate authors, in time for the next edition – and the most useful submissions are rewarded with a free book. To send us your updates – and find out about Lonely Planet events, newsletters and travel news – visit our award-winning website: **www.lonelyplanet.com/feedback**.

Note: We may edit, reproduce and incorporate your comments in Lonely Planet products such as guidebooks, websites and digital products, so let us know if you don't want your comments reproduced or your name acknowledged. For a copy of our privacy policy visit **www.lonelyplanet.com/privacy**.

Introducing Ljubljana

Where oh where have you been hiding, Ljubljana? Is it really possible that this absolutely gorgeous little capital – whose name means 'beloved' *(ljubljena)* in Slovenian – has escaped detection by the all-pervasive European tourist radar until now? The adventurers and trail-blazers may scoff and talk knowingly of Ljubljana's stunning historic core, atmospherically wrapped around the lazy bends of the Ljubljanica beneath the watchful gaze of a hilltop castle, but that's the whole point: they're the only ones who know about it.

Until recently, that is. In 2004, Slovenia – that tiny semi-Balkan, ex-Yugoslavian state – joined the EU, an inevitable step in the journey that began with the declaration of independence from the Yugoslav federation in 1991. It escaped the devastating wars that followed, but it was too close to the conflict and most of us too ignorant of the truth to venture forth and visit. More fools us, but all the better for what's on offer now that the city has opened itself to the world.

And everyone's gone gaga for Ljubljana. It may not have any world-class attractions, but it has a superb mix of architecture old and new that serves as the backdrop for its greatest crowd-pleaser – the street life that comes alive in summer, when café tables spill into the narrow streets of the Old Town and Ljubljana becomes a little Prague or Budapest minus the crowds or the hype.

Who would have thought that a small European capital could draw gasps of surprise from the jaded masses in these seen-it-all times? Come to Ljubljana and find out.

Stunning views from the Ljubljanica river

Neighbourhoods

Ljubljana (pronounced loo-blee-yana) is so small that getting around is a cinch. Within these small confines the city is traditionally divided into two dozen districts, but only a handful are of any importance to travellers.

At the heart of the city is the **Old Town**, running the length of the right bank of the Ljubljanica River. Flanking the narrow cobbled streets and narrow squares are Ljubljana's oldest and most beautiful baroque buildings and churches. The main drag is Mestni trg (*trg* is 'square' in Slovene) which narrows up and becomes Stari trg (which is more like a street); these two are lined with lovely cafés, bars and shops, as is the bank of the Ljubljanica, although they tend to be a little more touristy. Standing tall above the Old Town is **Castle Hill**, atop which sits…that's right, the castle.

The most famous bridge over the Ljubljanica is Jože Plečnik's Triple Bridge (Tromostovje), which leads to the city's most beautiful square – Prešernov trg – and **Center**, the commercial hub of town. Running north from the square is handsome Miklošičeva cesta, partly lined with elegant art nouveau buildings (as well as the city's swankiest hotel). To the west is Slovenska cesta, Center's main thoroughfare, packed with shops, shoppers and traffic.

West of Slovenska cesta along Tomisčeva ulica is the **parliament**, the small-but-significant **museum district** and the green expanse of Park Tivoli, Ljubljana's largest park by far.

To the south of Center are the gorgeous rural suburbs of **Krakovo** and **Trnovo** – two slices of village living divided by a lazy, narrow canal.

The railway and bus stations are north of Center and the Old Town along Masarykova ulica. East along this street is the old army barracks of **Metelkova**, now the hub of Ljubljana's alternative art scene and nightlife. Immediately south of here are the two largely residential districts of **Tabor** and – just across the Ljubljanica once more into the Old Town – **Poljane**. North of the railway station is the modern suburb of **Bežigrad**, where the bulk of the university buildings are, lined along Dunajska cesta (so-called because it's the main road to Dunaj, or Vienna).

PEDESTRIANISED LJUBLJANA

Certain streets and squares (eg Čopova ulica, Prešernov trg, most of Trubarjeva cesta) and much of the Old Town are reserved for pedestrians. The Ljubljanica is crossed by more than a dozen vehicular bridges and footbridges, and three of them – Cobbler Bridge (Čevljarski most), Dragon Bridge (Zmajski most) and of course Triple Bridge (Tromostovje) – are historically important.

Itineraries

Small, compact and crammed with handsome buildings, cobbled streets and pleasant squares, Ljubljana serves up a mini-feast of medieval, baroque and Secessionist delights for visitors to enjoy at their leisure – not to mention a café- and pub-life that will stall even the most intrepid walkers.

DAY ONE

First things first: a coffee at **Kavarna Pločnik** (p38) on **Prešernov trg** (p8). Cross **Triple Bridge** (p8) to Mestni trg and begin a tour of the Old Town. Ascend Ulica na Grad from Gornji trg to **Ljubljana Castle** and the **Virtual Museum** (p9). Walk down the hill back to Stari trg and get stuck into some Slovenian tucker at **Gostilna Pri Pavli** (p30). In the afternoon visit the **National Museum of Contemporary History** (p12) or the **National Gallery** (p11) and then walk through **Park Tivoli** (p10) to cool off (or warm up – depending on the season) at the **Tivoli Recreation Centre** (p54) with a swim or a sauna. Sample some Serbian cuisine at **Pod Rožnikom** (p36) before stopping by **Čarli** (p37) for a late drink.

DAY TWO

Take the **TIC (tourist office) walking tour** (p25) for an introduction to the unusual architectural contributions of Jože Plečnik. After lunch at **Pri Škofu** (p35), rent or borrow one of the free bikes on offer from **Ljubljana Bike** (p54) and cycle through Park Tivoli to the **Ljubljana Zoo** (p21) or along the Ljubljanica River. In the evening take in a performance at the **Križanke** (p42) or **Cankarjev Dom** (p42) or visit one of the clubs in **Metelkova** (p40).

Ljubljana Castle (p9) towers above the Old Town

Highlights

PREŠERNOV TRG (4, D4)

The centrepiece of Ljubljana's wonderful architectural aesthetic is this marvellous square, a public space of understated elegance that not only serves as the link between Center and the Old Town but as the city's favourite meeting point.

The square itself is dominated by a monument to the poet France Prešeren (p50). It was designed by Maks Fabiani and Ivan Zajc and erected in 1905 – its centenary celebrations in October 2005 were a packed, two-day affair of music, dancing and eulogy, proof that Slovenes don't mess about when paying tribute to their greatest poet. The plinth is adorned with motifs from his poems.

HE LOVES ME, I LOVE HIM NOT...

Two doors down from the Ura building, at Wolfova ulica 4, is a terracotta figure peeking out from a 'window'. It's a relief of one Julija Primic (1816–64), who met France Prešeren in the Church of St John the Baptist (p13) in Trnovo one Sunday in 1833. He was twice her age and in a life-long relationship with booze, but he was so smitten with the young girl that she became his poetic muse and the object of his unrequited love. She scorned him while he was alive but he eventually got his wish, if only in immortalised clay: her terracotta gaze is forever fixed on his monument in the middle of the square.

Immediately south of the statue is the city's architectural poster-child, the small but much celebrated Triple Bridge (Tromostovje). The original Špital Bridge (1842) was nothing spectacular, but between 1929 and 1932 superstar architect Jože Plečnik (p50) added the two pedestrian side bridges, furnished all three with stone balustrades and lamps and forced a name change. Stairways on each of the side bridges lead down to the poplar-lined terraces along the Ljubljanica River (as well as the cleanest public toilets we've ever seen in Europe!).

To the east of the monument, at Presemov trg 5, is the Italianate Central Pharmacy (Centralna Lekarna), once a café frequented by intellectuals in the 19th century, and to the north, on the corner of Trubarjeva cesta and Miklošičeva cesta, is the delightful Secessionist Urbanc building (1903), now the Centromerkur department store. Diagonally across the square at No 1 is another Secessionist gem: the Hauptman House (or Ura building), once a shop for painters and hence very gaily decorated.

And what of the big pink church on the northern side? See p18 to find out.

The much photographed, much loved Triple Bridge

LJUBLJANA CASTLE (4, D5)

Dominating the Old Town and visible from pretty much everywhere in Ljubljana is Ljubljana Castle (Ljubljanski Grad), which crowns an abrupt, wooded hill. Although there have been fortifications on this vantage point at least since Celtic times (it was inhabited as far back as 1200 BC), the current fort dates largely from a 16th-century reconstruction following the earthquake of 1511. It was a royal residence in the 17th and 18th centuries and a prison and barracks in the 19th and first half of the 20th centuries.

INFORMATION

- ☎ 232 99 94
- 🖥 www.festival-lj.si
- € castle free; Virtual Museum 1100/790SIT
- 🕑 castle 9am-10pm May-Sep, 10am-9pm Oct-Apr; Virtual Museum 9am-9pm May-Sep, 10am-6pm Oct-Apr; Pentagonal Tower 10am-7pm
- ℹ guided tours (1100/800SIT) 10am & 4pm daily, Jun–mid-Sep from bridge at castle entrance
- 🚌 tourist train (turistični vlak) from Prešernov Trg; 600/400SIT return; 🕑 10am-8pm

The castle's main highlight is the 19th-century Pentagonal Tower. The viewing platform, 95 wrought-iron steps from the bottom, offers vertiginous, 360-degree views of the city and surrounding countryside. At the base of the tower is the relatively new **Virtual Museum**, where you don your 3-D glasses and audio guide (available in four languages) and travel through the main (albeit badly described) epochs of Ljubljana's history (p47) before coming to a stuttering halt in 1991 and the declaration of independence.

You can reach the castle from the Old Town via three routes: Študentovska ulica, which runs south from Ciril-Metodov trg; steep Reber ulica from Stari trg; and Ulica na Grad from Gornji trg. If you don't fancy the climb, you can always opt for the 'tourist train' (really a conjoined bus) that departs on the hour from Prešernov Trg and goes back down again at 20 minutes past the hour from the castle gates.

Castle tours depart from the bridge at the castle's main entrance and include admission to the tower and the museum.

A bit of a climb but worth it for fabulous views over the city

DISCOUNT CARD

Visitors would do well to invest in the **Ljubljana Card** (3000SIT for 72 hours), which gives free or reduced entry to all of the city's museums as well as a host of other perks, such as complimentary drinks in certain restaurants, shopping discounts and free public transport. It is available from all tourist offices.

PARK TIVOLI (3, A2)

Ljubljana's oversized green lung is a huge, leafy playground measuring 5sq km that clings tightly to the edge of the city centre; one of its many entrances is just a 10-minute walk from Prešernov Trg. Inside you'll find sporting facilities, cafés and museums – including the excellent **National Museum of Contemporary History** (see p12) – spread about the formal landscapes originally laid out in 1813.

The main entrance, via the underpass at the western end of Cankarjeva cesta, opens onto Jakopičevo sprehajališče at the end of which is the monumental Jakopič Promenade designed by Plečnik in the 1920s and '30s. Here is the 17th-century Tivoli Mansion (3, B3; Tivolski Grad), which now contains the **International Centre of Graphic Arts** (Mednarodni Grafični Likovni Center, or MGLC). With new exhibitions every three months, the centre also hosts the International Biennial of Graphic Arts in odd-numbered years (see p43).

The **Ljubljana Zoo** lies on the southern slope of Rožnik Hill, and if caged animals don't float your boat, Rožnik Hill (394m) is a hiker's dream, with a decent climbing path to the top, where you can recuperate with some excellent food.

INFORMATION
☎ 241 38 18 (MGLC) ⌨ www.mglc-lj.si (MGLC) ✉ Pod turnom 3 (MGLC)
€ 800/400SIT (MGLC) ☽ 11am-6pm Wed-Sun (MGLC)
✖ Gostilna Rožnik (p36)

DON'T MISS
• A clamber up Rožnik Hill
• The National Museum of Contemporary History (p12)
• Lunch and a beer at Gostilna Rožnik (p36)

NATIONAL GALLERY (4, B3)

INFORMATION
- ☎ 241 54 34
- 🖥 www.ng-slo.si
- ✉ Prešernova ulica 24 & Puharjeva ulica 9
- € 1000/700SIT, free 2-6pm Sat
- 🕐 10am-6pm Tue-Sun

Slovenia's foremost collection of fine art is contained within the two buildings that make up the National Gallery (Narodna Galerija). The original Habsburg-era mansion, built in 1896 as the Slovenski Dom (National House) to host all manner of cultural events, is where you'll find portraits and Slovenian landscapes from the 17th to 19th centuries (check out works by 'national Romantics' Pavel Künl, Marko Pernhart and Anton Karinger) as well as copies of medieval frescoes and wonderful Gothic statuary. Although the subjects of the earlier paintings are the usual foppish nobles and lemon-lipped clergymen, some of the later works are remarkable and provide a good introduction to Slovenian art. Take a close look at the works of the Impressionists Jurij Šubic (eg *Before the Hunt*) and Rihard Jakopič *(Birches in Autumn)*, the Pointillist Ivan Grohar *(Škofja Loka in the Snow)* and Slovenia's most celebrated female painter Ivana Kobilca *(Summer)*. The bronzes by Franc Berneker and Anton Gangl are truly exceptional, and the 30-minute video installation *Secrets of the Soča* by Andrej Zdravič, in which the cobalt-blue river is viewed from the bottom up, is hypnotising.

DON'T MISS
- The Impressionist paintings
- Franc Berneker and Anton Gangl's wonderful bronzes
- The Gothic statuary

The gallery's permanent collection of European paintings from the Middle Ages to the present day is housed within the newish extension, a thoroughly postmodern addition linked to the older building via a glass walkway. It is also used for an ever-changing programme of temporary exhibits; check the website for what tends to be a pretty high-calibre menu of shows.

NATIONAL MUSEUM OF CONTEMPORARY HISTORY (3, B2)

The internal expanse of the 18th-century Cekin Mansion (Cekinov Grad), just northeast of the Tivoli Recreation Centre, is home to arguably Ljubljana's most interesting museum, the Musej Novejše Zgodovine Slovenije. Taking an intimate peek at Slovenia's turbulent history from the turn of the 20th century to the declaration of independence in 1991, it is refreshingly and unavoidably political, shirking little but skilfully managing not to fall on one side or another.

Its multimedia story begins on the eve of WWI, leading you through a surprisingly effective reconstruction of a typical trench into the quieter days of the post-war Kingdom of Yugoslavia. It gets pretty turbulent once more in Room E, which deals with WWII and the Italo-German occupation, but the museum's most fascinating exhibits deal with socialist Yugoslavia. Note the contrast between the sober earnestness of the communist-era Room G and the exuberant, logo-mad commercialism of the neighbouring industrial exhibit in Room H. A portrait of Stalin lies 'discarded' behind the door between the two. The gloriously baroque Ceremonial Hall (Room F) gives an idea of how the whole mansion once looked.

The ground floor is used for equally fascinating temporary exhibits; one such display in late 2005 listed the name of every single Ljubljana member of the right-leaning anti-communist Home Guard summarily executed by Partisan fighters in the latter years of WWII. Considering the swing to the right of the current Slovene government, it is an appropriately incendiary exhibit.

INFORMATION

- ☎ 300 96 10
- 🖥 www.muzej-nz.si
- ✉ Celovška cesta 23
- € 800/600SIT; free first Sun of the month
- 🕐 10am-6pm
- ♿ fair

DON'T MISS

- The Socialist Pantry (Room G)
- The Ceremonial Hall (Room F)
- The WWI trench (Room B)

KRAKOVO & TRNOVO (2)

More like little country villages than inner-city suburbs, the distinct neighbourhoods of Krakovo and Trnovo are among Ljubljana's prettiest, crossed by narrow streets lined with gorgeous two-storey cottages and dotted with perfectly tended vegetable patches whose produce fill the stalls at the daily market (p26) on Vodnikov trg. Although Trnovo, immediately south of the Gradaščica Canal, has a couple of interesting sights worth exploring, Krakovo is the more atmospheric of the two neighbourhoods. You'll get a real sense of its character just strolling the shortish length of Krakovska ulica, staring through the gates into the beguiling little courtyards that front most of the houses on the street.

If you need a little history, the substantial Roman wall (2, A1) running along Mirje from Barjanska cesta dates from AD 15; the archway topped with a pyramid is a Plečnik addition. Within the **Jakopič Garden** (2, A2) to the southeast, where the Impressionist painter Rihard Jakopič once worked in his summerhouse, there are more Roman remains, including household artefacts, mosaics and the vestiges of sophisticated heating and sewage systems. Ask the Cultural & Information Centre (p57) about access to the garden.

INFORMATION

☎ 283 50 60 (church)

✉ Mirje 4 (Jakopič Garden); Kolezijska ulica 1 (Church of St John the Baptist)

€ free (garden & church)

DON'T MISS
- Courtyards and alleyways
- Well-tended vegetable plots
- The Plečnik Collection
- Plečnik's lovely Trnovo Bridge

Spanning the picturesque Gradaščica Canal is little Trnovo Bridge, designed in 1932 by Plečnik, who added five of his trademark pyramids. Immediately south of the bridge is the **Church of St John the Baptist** (Cerkev Sv Janeza Krstnika), where France Prešeren first met Julija Primic, the unrequited love of his life (p8). Plečnik undoubtedly had happier memories of the place, for he lived and worked for almost 40 years only a few steps south of the church. His former dwelling now houses the Plečnik Collection (p16).

NATIONAL MUSEUM & NATURAL HISTORY MUSEUM (4, B4)

Bright and sparkling thanks to a recent renovation, this elegant 1885 building, designed in the Czech art nouveau style known as Rudolfinum, is probably more impressive than the collections it contains. Beyond the four allegorical figures – Art, History, Natural History and Labour – that grace the entrance and the stunning foyer, with its ceiling fresco depicting important Slovenians from the past and statues of the Muses and Fates relaxing on the stone stairway banisters, is some pretty standard fare. The National Museum (Narodni Muzej Slovenije) boasts the only Egyptian mummy in Slovenia, and the Roman glass and the jewellery found in 6th-century Slavic graves is pretty enough, but the highlight here is the highly embossed Vače situla, a Celtic pail from the late 6th century BC unearthed in a town east of Ljubljana.

The Natural History Museum (Prirodoslovni Muzej Slovenije) contains the usual reassembled mammoth and whale skeletons, stuffed birds, reptiles and mammals. Worth a visit, however, are the mineral collections amassed by the philanthropic Baron Žiga Zois in the early 19th century and the display on Slovenia's unique salamander *Proteus anguinus*, found in caves like Postojna (p24).

INFORMATION

- ☎ 241 44 04 National Museum; 241 09 40 Natural History Museum
- 🖳 www.narmuz-lj.si National Museum; www.pms-lj.si Natural History Museum
- ✉ Prešernova 20; entrance at Muzejska ulica 1
- € 700/500SIT; combination ticket 1100/800SIT; free first Sun of the month
- ☯ 10am-6pm, 10am-8pm Thu

DON'T MISS

- 300 different kinds of birds in the Natural History Museum
- The pickled poisonous snakes in jars
- The stunning neo-Renaissance museum building

METELKOVA (3, E3)

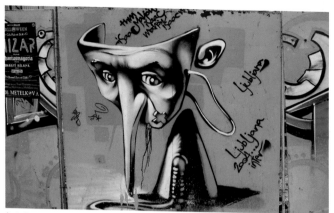

Artistic expression extends to the walls in Metelkova

By day, this former army garrison, abandoned by the Yugoslav Army after independence, is nothing much to look at, just a bunch of rundown buildings speckled with graffiti. By night, however, it comes alive in a flurry of alternative activity, for Metelkova Mesto – to give it its full name – is one of the most vibrant cultural hives you'll find anywhere, a free-living commune that is a miniature version of Copenhagen's Christiania.

Its radically alternative bent is somewhat daunting at first – many would think twice before approaching a group of pierced punks drinking beer and smoking hash – but the spirit of Metelkova is first and foremost a culturally expressive one and the emphasis here is on art and music. The six buildings of the northern section of the one-time barracks put on an ever-changing show of art exhibits, gigs, clubs, readings and other such artistic fare.

NIGHT OWLS

If you're going to Metelkova for an art exhibit, anytime in the evening and early night will do; if you're going for a gig or a club night, don't bother showing up before midnight or 1am.

There's something on most nights, but it really gets going Thursday through Saturday nights, when you can dance, drink and smoke until the very, very wee hours. If you happen to be here during the day, you will find everything closed except for the ultrahip Celica Hostel (see p46), which is so cool that there are guided tours of the place.

Needless to say, as Slovenia stretches further into prosperous independence, valuable real estate such as Metelkova has become highly prized by developers, and the whole project is under constant threat from the government. Naturally, there are petitions against it. Check out www.metelkova.org/indexe.htm for the latest developments and to register your protest, if you like.

Sights & Activities

MUSEUMS

Ljubljana's museums are stimulating, with plenty on offer from architecture to beer.

Architectural Museum
(3, off F3)

The museum (Arhitekturni Muzej Ljubljana) should really be called the Plečnik Show, as the mainstay of the permanent collection is the great man's Paris Exhibition and other displays of his work.
☎ 540 97 98 🖳 www.arhmuz.com ✉ Fužine Castle, Pot na Fužine 2, Studenec € 500/300SIT 🕓 10am-2pm Mon-Fri 🚌 20 to Fužine 🦽 good

Brewery Museum
(4, B1)

Beer-making displays in the museum (Pivovarksi Muzej) and a tour of Ljubljana's Union Brewery.
☎ 471 73 40 🖳 www.pivo-union.si ✉ Pivovarniška ulica 2 € free 🕓 8am-1pm 1st Tue of month & by appointment 🦽 good

City Museum (1, C6)

A collection of well-preserved Roman artefacts (some of them recovered from a dig in the museum courtyard) and a scale model of the Roman town of Emona are the highlights of the City Museum (Mestni Muzej), housed in what was once the Auersberg Palace. It has just reopened after a major redesign and is still something of a work in progress.
☎ 426 35 67 🖳 www.mm-lj.si ✉ Gosposka ulica 15 € free 🕓 10am-6pm Tue-Sun 🦽 good

Museum of Modern Art
(4, A3)

The outwardly drab 1940s Museum of Modern Art (Moderna Galerija) exhibits a permanent collection of inspiring 20th-century Slovenian art – lots of Surrealism, Expressionism and multimedia.
☎ 251 41 06 🖳 www.mg-lj.si ✉ Cankarjeva cesta 15 € 1000/700SIT 🕓 10am-6pm Tue-Sat, to 1pm Sun 🦽 good

Plečnik Collection
(2, A3)

The collection in the house where the almost ascetically religious architect Jože Plečnik lived and worked for 40 years is an excellent introduction to his inspirations and his work.
☎ 283 50 67 ✉ Karunova ulica 4 € 1000/500SIT 🕓 10am-2pm & 4-6pm Tue & Thu, guided tours hourly 10am-1pm & 4-5pm

Railway Museum
(3, off D1)

Steam locomotives, coaches and other rolling stock are displayed at this museum (Železniški Muzej). Perfect for trainspotters and their patient grandkids, with lots of train paintings too.
☎ 291 26 41 🖳 www.burger.si/MuzejiInGalerije/ZelezniskiMuzej ✉ Parmova

Quiet contemplation in the Museum of Modern Art

ulica 35 € 500/200SIT
🕑 10am-6pm Tue-Sun
🚋 11, 21 to Parmova ulica

Slovenian Ethnographic Museum (3, D3)

A fascinating exploration of Slovenian ethnology and of the folk cultures and mores of other countries is the theme of this newly refurbished museum (Slovenski Etnografski Muzej) in the heart of Metelkova.
☎ 432 54 03 🖳 www.etno-muzej.si ✉ Metelkova ulica 2 € 800/500SIT 🕑 10am-6pm Tue-Sun 🚻 good

Slovenian School Museum (4, B5)

Founded in 1898, this museum (Slovenski Šolski Muzej) is dedicated to how Slovenian kids learned the three Rs over the centuries. Lots of plastic models and dioramas with explanations in Slovenian.
☎ 251 30 24 🖳 www.ssolski-muzej.si ✉ Plečnikov trg 1 € free 🕑 9am-1pm Mon-Fri

Slovenian Theatre Museum (4, D5)

Slovenia's rich thespian tradition over the last two centuries is given the full treatment at this Old Town museum (Slovenski Gledališki Muzej), which is a must for anyone interested in the country's theatrical history.
☎ 241 58 00 🖳 sgm@guest.arnes.si
✉ Mestni trg 17
€ free 🕑 10am-1pm & 5-7pm Mon-Fri, mornings only Sat

Sports Museum (4, E5)

Slovenia is pretty good at some sports, especially the ones that involve strapping on skis and going quickly down mountains and over land. This new museum (Muzej Športa) looks at that history.
☎ 431 83 40 🖳 iztok11dur@voljanet
✉ Kopitarjeva ulica 2-4 € free 🕑 10am-1pm Mon-Fri

Technical Museum of Slovenia (1, B2)

A full and worthwhile day out 22km southwest of Ljubljana at the Tehniški Mujez Slovenije, with its huge collection of antique motor vehicles and bicycles, water-driven and horse-powered mills, all housed within the confines of the elegant Bistra Castle.
☎ 750 66 70 🖳 www.tms.si ✉ Bistra Castle, Bistra, near Vrhnika € 700/500SIT 🕑 8am-6pm Tue-Sun Jul-Aug (guided tours on the hr), 8am-4pm Tue-Fri, 9am-5pm Sat, 10am-6pm Sun rest of yr 🚌 bus to Vrhnika or trains to Verd

Tobacco Museum (3, B4)

Ljubljana's first factory is home to this fascinating museum (Tobačni Muzej) devoted to the questionable pleasure of tobacco, from how it's grown to how it's turned into the stuff you smoke – with ne'er a mention of the health risks!
☎ 477 73 44 🖳 www.tobacna.si ✉ Tobacco Factory, Tobačna ulica 5 € free 🕑 10am-6pm 1st Wed & 3rd Thu of month 🚋 6 to Tobačna ulica

CHURCHES & CATHEDRALS

Ljubljana's largely baroque churches were kept intact throughout the socialist half-century of its history and are regularly attended today; indeed, their atmosphere is best enjoyed during services.

Church of St Florian (4, D6)

Built in 1672 after a blaze destroyed much of the Old Town, this church (Cerkev Sv Florijana) is appositely dedicated to the patron saint of fires.
☎ 252 17 27 ✉ Gornij trg 18 € free 🕑 7am-12.30pm & 3-8pm 🚻 good

Church of St James (4, D6)

Besides the main altar (1732) by Robba, the highlight of Cerkev Sv Jakoba is the Chapel of St Francis Xavier,

THE CITIZEN OF EMONA

As you descend the Plečnik underpass (Plečnikov podhod) at the western end of Kongresni trg to get to the Ursuline Church, you will see on your right a small gilt statue on top of a column. This is a copy (the original is in the National Museum) of a figure known as the Citizen of Emona, dating from the 4th century and unearthed nearby in 1836.

with statues of a 'White Queen' and a 'Black King'. ✉ Levstikov trg € free 🕐 7am-12.30pm & 3-8pm ♿ good

Franciscan Church of the Annunciation (4, D4)

Dominating Prešernov Trg's northern end is this pink church (Frančiškanska Cerkev Marijinega Oznanjanja), built between 1646 and 1660 in the Italianate style. The interior is not especially interesting, but to the left (west) of the main altar, designed by Francesco Robba (1698–1757), is a glass-fronted coffin with the spooky remains of St Deodatus, originally brought here by a monk in the early 18th century. ☎ 425 30 07 ✉ Prešernov trg 4 € free 🕐 6.45am-12.30pm & 3-8pm ♿ fair

St Nicholas' Cathedral (4, D4)

Ljubljana's 18th-century cathedral (*Stolnica*) is a baroque palace of pink marble, white stucco and gilding, with frescoes by baroque master Giulio Quaglio and 19th-century artist Matevž Langus. Have a look at the magnificent carved choir stalls, the organ and the angels on the main altar — another Robba creation. ☎ 231 06 84

✉ Dolničarjeva ulica 1 € free 🕐 10am-noon & 3-6pm ♿ good

Serbian Orthodox Church (4, A3)

The interior of this 1936 church (Srbska Pravoslavna Cerkev) dedicated to St Cyril and St Methodius is covered from floor to ceiling with colourful modern frescoes. A richly carved iconostasis separates the nave from the sanctuary. ☎ 252 40 02 ✉ Prešernova cesta € free 🕐 2-6pm Tue-Sun ♿ excellent

Ursuline Church of the Holy Trinity (4, B5)

Ljubljana's most beautiful baroque building is this church (Uršulinska Cerkev Svete Trojice), dating from 1726. It contains a multicoloured altar by Robba made of African marble. ☎ 252 48 64 ✉ Slovenska cesta 21 € free 🕐 9-10.30am & 4.30-7pm ♿ good

ART GALLERIES

For such a small capital, Ljubljana has an abundance of art galleries that display a panoply of work in all shapes and sizes, from classical to contemporary.

City Gallery (4, D5)

Rotating displays of contemporary art, sculpture, graphics and conceptual pieces in a municipal art gallery in the heart of the Old Town. ☎ 241 17 70 🖳 www.mestna-galerija.si, in Slovenian only ✉ Mestni

Pretty in pink: the Franciscan Church of the Annunciation

trg 5 € free ☼ 10am-6pm
Tue-Sat, 10am-1pm Sun

DESSA Architectural Gallery (4, C5)
Small gallery spotlighting
contemporary Slovenian
architecture and architects
as well as the work of
international architects.
There's also a research
archive on site.
☎ 251 60 10 ☐ www2.
arnes.si/~ljdessa1
✉ Židovska steza 4 € free
☼ 10am-3pm Mon-Fri

Galerija Equrna (4, B6)
Ljubljana's most exciting
contemporary gallery is in a
pleasant courtyard marked
by a large blue banner.
Exhibitions change every
four weeks or so and focus
primarily on Slovenian
artists.
☎ 252 71 23 ☐ equrna@
siol.net ✉ Gregorčičeva
ulica 3 € free ☼ 10am-
2pm & 5-7pm Mon-Fri,
10am-1pm Sat

Luwigiana Gallery (4, D6)
This well-respected gallery
in the Old Town displays and
sells the work of both local
and international artists; it's
not especially cutting-edge,
but the work is of a very high
quality.
☎ 252 73 69 ✉ Gornji trg
19 € free ☼ 11am-7pm
Mon-Fri, 10am-1pm Sat
♿ excellent

ŠKUC Gallery (4, D6)
The Students' Cultural and
Arts Centre (ŠKUC) runs this
provocative, avant-garde art
gallery in the heart of the Old
Town featuring the new work
of up-and-coming local artists.

Dogged by difficult choices in the Luwigiana Gallery

☎ 421 31 40 ☐ www.
galerija.skuc-drustvo.si
✉ Stari trg 21
€ free ☼ noon-8pm
Tue-Sun

Small Gallery (4, C3)
Contemporary artists from
Slovenia and elsewhere
exhibit their cutting-edge
work in this fairly compact
space, hence its name (Mala
Galerija).
☎ 241 68 00 ☐ www.
mg-lj.si ✉ Slovenska cesta
35 € free ☼ 11am-6pm
Tue-Sat, 10am-1pm Sun

NOTABLE BUILDINGS

The best streets for admir-
ing Ljubljana's architecture
are Miklošičeva cesta, which
runs north from Prešernov
trg and at the southern
end of which are a host of
Secessionist classics; and the
Old Town's main thorough-
fare, made up of Mestni trg,
Stari trg and Gornij trg.

Abecedarium Café (4, D5)
A small passageway to the
right of Trubarjev Antikvariat
(p28) leads west into tiny
Ribji trg (Fish Square) where
Ljubljana's oldest house
still stands at No 2. It was
built in 1528 and is now a
very popular café-bar (p39).
Check out the building and
the excellent coffee at the
same time.
✉ Ribji trg 2

THE FOUNTAIN THAT ISN'T
One of Ljubljana's most
famous monuments
is the baroque Robba
Fountain (1751), which
is located directly in
front of the Town Hall.
It was removed for
cleaning and repair in
2004, leaving the base
covered in see-through
Perspex. It should be
back up in its place by
the end of 2006.

Cooperative Business Bank Building (4, D4)

The old Cooperative Bank, the Zadružna Gospodarska Banka, has the city's most distinctive facade. It was the work of artist Helena Vurnik, who added the red, yellow and blue geometric patterns to the building, designed by her husband Ivan in 1922.

✉ Miklošičeva cesta 8
☯ closed to the public

Gruber Palace (2, C1)

This handsome building (Gruberjeva Palača) is named after Gabriel Gruber, the Jesuit who built the canal (Gruberjev Prekop) that regulates the Ljubljanica and who lived here until 1784. The palace is in Zopf style, a transitional style between late baroque and neoclassical, and now contains the national archives.

✉ Zvezdarska ulica 1
☯ closed to the public

THIS IS NOT A WHOREHOUSE!
It's not accidental that Schweiger House has no number – in this part of the world, bordellos were usually located at No 13. No wonder the figure on the building is asking for a little quiet!

People's Loan Bank (4, D4)

Built in 1908, this cream-coloured bank (Slovenska Zadružna Kmetijska Banka) is topped with the figures of two women holding a beehive and a purse, symbols of industry and wealth.

✉ Miklošičeva cesta 4
☯ closed to the public

Schweiger House (4, D6)

On Stavi trg is a lovely rococco building known as Schweiger House. A large figure of Atlas supports the upper balcony: he has his finger raised to his lips as if asking passers-by to be quiet.

✉ Stari trg, btwn 11a & 15 ☯ closed to the public

Town Hall (4, D5)

Ljubljana's town hall (rotovž) is the seat of the city's government and is sometimes refered to as the Magistrat. It was erected in the late 15th century and rebuilt in 1718. The Gothic courtyard inside, arcaded on two levels, once hosted theatrical performances. The building is topped with Ljubljana's symbol, a dragon (p47).

☎ 306 30 00 ✉ Mestni trg € free ☯ 9am-9pm Mon-Fri ⚹ excellent

SQUARES

Prešernov trg (p8) is the city's most famous central gathering place, but there are a couple of other squares that are just as beautiful, even if they don't look much like squares.

Kongresni trg (4, C4)

Named in honour of the Congress of the Holy Alliance, convened by Austria, Prussia, Russia and Naples in 1821 and hosted by Ljubljana, this lovely square with a park in the centre is called Zvezda (Star) because of the shape in which the decorative trees were planted.

Stari trg (4, D5)

Its name means 'Old Square', but it's really more of a cobbled street, lined with 19th-century

The brightly patterned façade of the old Cooperative Bank

wooden shop fronts and quiet courtyards and with cobblestone passageways leading off it. At what is now No 4 a prison called Tranča stood until the 18th century, and those condemned to death were executed at a spot nearby.

Trg Francoske Revolucije (4, B6)

One of Ljubljana's loveliest public spaces is French Revolution Square. It is lined with elegant buildings and in the centre is the Ilirija Column. The monument is dedicated to Napoleon and the Illyrian Provinces (1809–13) that he created (p47). This was when Slovene was taught in schools for the first time.

Vodnikov trg (4, E4)

Ljubljana's fabulous central market takes place every day except Sunday. Ljubljančani stock up on everything here, from delicious comestibles to flowers and clothing. Fresh fruit and veg, mouthwatering gourmet tidbits from mushrooms to homemade cheese make this market a foodie dream.

BRIDGES

Apart from the renowned Triple Bridge (p8), the Ljubljanica river is crossed by a couple of other notable structures.

Treat the kids to a donkey ride in Park Tivoli (p10)

Cobbler Bridge (4, C5)

Like all medieval bridges, Cobbler Bridge (Šustarski most) was a place of trade. Craftsmen (in this case 16 shoemakers) worked and lived on the bridge to catch the traffic and avoid paying town taxes – a kind of medieval duty-free set-up.

Dragon Bridge (4, E4)

In the early 20th century a wily mayor apparently persuaded the authorities in Vienna that Ljubljana needed a new crossing over the Ljubljanica, and Dragon Bridge (Zmajski most) was built to the northeast, off Vodnikov trg.

LJUBLJANA FOR CHILDREN

Ljubljana Zoo (3, off A3)

The 45ha Ljubljana Zoo (Živalski Vrt Ljubljana), on the southern slope of Rožnik Hill, contains 500 animals representing 120 species. There's also a petting zoo which the kids should enjoy. ☎ 244 21 88 ☐ www. zoo-ljubljana.si, Slovene only ✉ Večna pot 70 € 1300/ 900SIT ⏱ 9am- 7pm May-Aug, 9am-6pm Apr & Sep, 9am-5pm Mar & Oct, 9am-4pm rest of year

---

VIRGINS AFOOT

City folk say the bronze dragons on Dragon Bridge wag their tails whenever a virgin crosses it – so far, absolutely nothing.

Trips & Tours

WALKING TOUR

Kick off in **Prešernov trg** (**1**; p8) at the heart of the city. Cross the famous **Triple Bridge** (**2**; p8) and take a left at the tourist office for a slow detour through the **Central Market** (**3**; p26) and its wonderful stalls and Pležnik's elegant colonnades. Take a right on Ciril-Metodov trg and walk back towards the Old Town, popping into the **cathedral** (**4**; p18) before crossing onto the cobblestones of Mestni trg. Past the impressive **town hall** (**5**; p20), explore the narrow lanes that lead down to the river from the square before continuing on down Stari trg, where you should get your choice of teas in the gorgeous **Čajna Hiša** (**6**; p39) before getting an eyeful of contemporary art at the **ŠKUC Gallery** (**7**; p19). Walk to the end of the street and take a right onto Karlovška cesta, crossing the Ljubljanica. Walk left along the river and take a right on to Krakovska ulica. You're in the heart of **Krakovo** (**8**; p13) a city neighbourhood more like a country neighbourhood – just check out all those vegetable patches. Peek through the gates at the atmospheric courtyards before finishing off with a bite at **Pri Škofu** (**9**; p35) on Rena ulica.

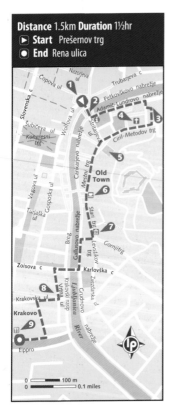

Ljubljana's imposing town hall (p20)

DAY TRIPS

Bled (1, B1)

With its shimmering, 2km-long subalpine lake, castle crag and romantic, church-laden island invitingly in the middle, Bled is the kind of idyllic spot you'd most likely see in a period film where the genteel classes of the 19th century come for an extended holiday. They did, and their present-day equivalents still do, in their tens of thousands. Slovenia's number one tourist destination is worth every effort to get to, even if the town itself is nothing special and in summer the whole place is overrun with coach tours.

> **INFORMATION**
>
> *54km northwest of Ljubljana*
> 🚐 A2 to Bled (45-60 min)
> 🚆 TIC (4, D3; ☎ 574 11 22; www.bled.si; 🕙 9am-6pm Mon-Sat, noon-5pm Sun, later in summer)
> 🍴 Penzion Mayer (5, E2; ☎ 04 574 10 58, www.mayer-sp.si, Želeška cesta 7, Bled)

Bled's photogenic trademark is the tiny island of Blejski Otok, with the baroque **Church of the Assumption** (5, B3; 🕙 8am-dusk, variable in winter). Getting there by piloted *plenta* (gondola; €14 per person, 1½ hours return) is the archetypal tourist experience.

Topping a sheer 100m-cliff, **Bled Castle** (Blejski Grad; 5, D1; ☎ 578 05 25; 1200/1100SIT; 🕙 8am-8pm May-Sep, 8am-5pm Oct-Apr) is the perfect backdrop to lake views, notably those from Mlino, on the lake's southern shore.

Hidden away in its own lakeside park beyond Mlino is **Vila Bled** (5, C3; ☎ 579 15 00; www.vila-bled.com; Cesta Svobode 26). This elegant villa is now a Relais & Châteaux hotel, but it started life as Tito's summer retreat.

The best way to enjoy Bled is to walk the 6km circuit around the lake. It should take around two hours, including the short, steep climb to the brilliant **Osojnica viewpoint** (5, A4).

Another popular, easy walk is to and through the 1.6km-long **Vintgar Gorge** (5, off E1; 600/400SIT; 🕙 May-Oct) along the century-old wooden walkway (no bicycles) which crisscrosses the fizzing Radovna River. The gorge is about 4.5km northwest of the lake.

The beautiful island of Blejski Otok

Postojna Cave & Predjama Castle (1, B3)

The stunning stalagmites and stalactites of **Postojna Cave** (1, B3; ☎ 700 01 00; www.postojnska -jama.si; 3700/2200SIT; guided tours hourly 9am-6pm May-Sep, every 2hrs 10am-4pm Oct-Apr) stretch endlessly in all directions, as do the chattering crowds who shuffle past them. A visit involves a 1.7km walk, with some gradients but

no steps. It culminates in a quick encounter with a cute salamander, *Proteus anguinus* or 'human-fish'. The very jolly highlight which both starts and finishes the tour is chugging between the limestone formations on an underground train. Dress warmly or hire a coat (700SIT): inside it's always cold.

Subterranean snacks at Postojna Cave's café

The caves are an unlikely venue for seasonal concerts and other such goings-on; at Christmas time a substantial Nativity scene is set up and the atmosphere is enhanced by actors and singers – the echo is quite incredible.

Idyllic **Predjama Castle** (1, B3; ☎ 700 01 00; adult/student 1100/830SIT; ☼ 10am-4pm Jan-Mar & Nov-Dec, 10am-6pm Apr & Oct, 9am-7pm May-Sep), only 9km northwest of Postojna, appears to grow out of a yawning cave.

Škofja Loka (1, B2)

A mere 25km northwest of Ljubljana is the bustling town of Škofja Loka. At its heart is the 1000-year-old Old Town, probably the most beautifully preserved medieval burg in Slovenia. The name means 'Bishop's Meadow' and for over 800 years the town was the personal property of the bishops of Freising. The Old Town is centred around the gorgeous Mestni trg, whose colourful 16th-century burgher houses have earned the town the nickname of 'Painted Loka'. Overlooking the town is Loški Grad, a 13th-century castle

that contains an interesting **ethnographic museum** (☎ 04-517 04 00; www.loski-muzej.si; Grajska pot 13; 600/400SIT; ☼ 9am-6pm Tue-Sun Apr-Oct, 9am-5pm Sat-Sun Nov-Mar).

The castle offers great views over the town of Škofja Loka

ORGANISED TOURS

You can see Ljubljana on foot, by bike, by river and from the air. The tourist office (p57) can also organise theme-specific tours, such as the baroque city or Plečnik's Ljubljana.

Boat Tour (4, C4)
It's an hour-long romantic wander down the Ljubljanica, passing all the main sights and beneath the city's most famous bridges.
☎ 306 12 15 🖳 www.ljubljana-tourism.si
✉ Ribji trg pier € 1000/500SIT ☿ check with TIC for schedule

Cycling Tour (4, E4)
See the city as most of its inhabitants experience it: by bike in one of the safest cycling cities in Europe. A helmet is included!
☎ 306 45 75 🖳 www.slovenia-tourism.si
✉ departs from Slovenian Tourist Office, Krekov trg 10
€ 3000SIT ☿ tours by appointment

Hot Air Balloon Flight (4, E4)
See Ljubljana and the surrounding countryside from up on high; the hour-long flight (of a total of four hours transfer and prep) is celebrated with a glass of sparkling wine.
☎ 306 45 75
🖳 www.slovenia-tourism.si
✉ departs from Slovenian Tourist Office, Krekov trg 10

€ 19,800/9900SIT
☿ 7am & 6pm daily Apr-Aug, 8am & 5pm daily Sep-Mar

Walking Tour (4, D5)
Two-hour tours of all the major sights of Center and the Old Town; also included is a 20-minute boat trip on the Ljubljanica River.
☎ 306 12 15 🖳 www.ljubljana-tourism.si
✉ departs from Town Hall
€ 1500/700SIT ☿ 10am daily May-Sep, 11am Fri-Sun Oct-Apr

A bike is one of the best ways to see the city

Shopping

Ljubljana is not what you'd call a shopper's paradise. For one, it's not that big a city, so the choice isn't as vast as you might find in other capitals.

MARKETS

Ljubljana's markets are one of its biggest attractions, especially at weekends, when everyone dresses up to prod fruit, test vegetables and check for woodworm in antique bric-a-brac.

Antiques Flea Market (4, D5)
Ljubljana's famous Sunday flea market offers antiques, art pieces and a variety of other items of collectable or simply nostalgic value – most notably anything associated with socialist Yugoslavia, like grey-green army uniforms, flags and photographs of Tito.
✉ Cankarjevo nabrežje
⌚ 8am-2pm Sun

Central Market (Tržnica) (4, E4)
At this wonderful open-air central market (Tržnica) old men and women sell everything from wild mushrooms and forest berries to honey and home-made cheeses, such as soft white *sirček*. The liveliest time is Saturday morning before noon.
☎ 300 12 00 ⌨ www.holdingljubljana.si/trznice ✉ Vodnikov trg & Pogačarjev trg ⌚ 6am-6pm Mon-Fri, to 4pm Sat Apr-Sep, 6am-4pm Mon-Sat Oct-Mar

Ljubljana Montmartre (4, E4)
During the summer months, the Central Market surrenders the square to this excellent arts and crafts market, which includes creative workshops for kids.

✉ Pogačarjev trg ⌚ 9am-4pm Sat Jun-Sep

SHOPPING CENTRES

Like almost everywhere else, Ljubljana has been struck down with mega-mall fever, where shopping is easy and done on a large scale.

BTC City (3, off F1)
With scores of large shops this sprawling mall in Moste, northeast of Center, is proof that 21st-century capitalism is just as soulless as it is convenient. The mall is constantly growing, with retail outlets being added almost weekly. It is also full of bars, cafés, restaurants and Ljubljana's only multiplex cinema.
☎ 585 14 56 ⌨ www.btc-city.com ✉ Šmartinska cesta 152 ⌚ 9am-9pm Mon-Sat, 9am-6pm Sun
🚌 2, 7, 17 🅿

DEPARTMENT STORES

A bunch of socialist-era leftovers have been given the capitalist once-over and are now indistinguishable from the department stores you'd find elsewhere.

Fabulous fresh produce at the Central Market

CLOTHING & SHOE SIZES

Women's Clothing

Aust/UK	8	10	12	14	16	18
Europe	36	38	40	42	44	46
Japan	5	7	9	11	13	15
USA	6	8	10	12	14	16

Women's Shoes

Aust/USA	5	6	7	8	9	10
Europe	35	36	37	38	39	40
France only	35	36	38	39	40	42
Japan	22	23	24	25	26	27
UK	3½	4½	5½	6½	7½	8½

Men's Clothing

Aust	92	96	100	104	108	112
Europe	46	48	50	52	54	56

Japan	S	M	M		L	
UK/USA	35	36	37	38	39	40

Men's Shirts (Collar Sizes)

Aust/Japan	38	39	40	41	42	43
Europe	38	39	40	41	42	43
UK/USA	15	15½	16	16½	17	17½

Men's Shoes

Aust/UK	7	8	9	10	11	12
Europe	41	42	43	44½	46	47
Japan	26	27	27.5	28	29	30
USA	7½	8½	9½	10½	11½	12½

Measurements approximate only; try before you buy.

BTC Emporium (3, off F1)
Part of BTC's retail megasprawl (see left), slightly upmarket and modern Emporium is the place to go for one-stop fashion shopping, with most major labels well represented for men, women and kids. ☎ 585 48 00 ✉ Letališka 3 ⏲ 10am-9pm Mon-Fri, 9am-8pm Sat, 10am-3pm Sun 🚌 2, 7, 17 🅿

Maximarket (4, B4)
You can buy pretty much anything in this large, centrally located department store; the basement has a sprawling supermarket (and is also a great spot to buy wine). ☎ 476 68 00 🖥 www.maxi.si, in Slovenian only ✉ Trg Republike 1 ⏲ 9am-9pm Mon-Fri, 8am-5pm Sat

ANTIQUES

There's a roaring trade in antiques in the city: if you're looking for something that little bit special to take home, it might well be an antique.

Antika Ferjan (4, D5)
Just inside an alleyway off Mestni trg and up a flight of stairs to the first floor is this largish shop. It specialises in pricey local and European antiques. ☎ 426 18 15 ✉ Mestni trg 21 ⏲ 9am-1pm & 3-7pm Mon-Fri, 9am-1pm Sat

Antikvariat Tizian (4, D5)
This Aladdin's Cave of curios and bric-a-brac is in an alleyway off Mestni trg. It is not quite as upmarket as other antique shops in the area. ☎ 426 71 41 ✉ Ključavničarska 3 ⏲ 10am-1pm & 5-8pm Mon-Fri, 10am-1pm Sat & Sun

Antikvitete Novak (4, C5)
This superb gallery has both old and new art and artefacts. You can walk out of here with goodies as different as an abstract oil painting or an elephant's foot ottoman. ☎ 426 65 41 ✉ Kongresni trg 1 ⏲ 10am-1pm & 4-7pm Mon-Fri, 10am-1pm Sat

Browse for bargains at the Antiques Flea Market (p26)

Carniola Antiqua (4, D4)
One of the city's best small
antiques galleries, Carniola's
collection is pretty diverse,
although it does a very good
line in art nouveau pieces.
☎ 231 63 97 ⊠ Trubarjeva
cesta 9 ⏰ 10am-1pm & 4-
7pm Mon-Fri, 10am-1pm Sat

Galerija Fortuna (4, D6)
Packed into this lovely shop
are some really beautiful
antiques, especially
glassware from the 1920s
and other delightful art
nouveau treasures. Prices are
pretty reasonable too.
☎ 425 01 87 ⊠ Stari trg
23 ⏰ 10am-1pm & 4-8pm
Mon-Fri, 10am-1pm Sat

Trubarjev Antikvariat
(4, D5)
Antiquarian and second-
hand books are the speciality
of this store. The books are
quite beautiful, but few of
them are in English – it helps
if your Slovenian and German
are up to speed.
☎ 244 26 83 ⊠ Mestni trg
25 ⏰ 8.30am-1pm & 5-8pm
Mon-Fri, 8.30am-1pm Sat &
4-7pm Sat Oct-May

FOLK ART & GIFTS

You can't go home without
checking out the work of

some of Ljubljana's truly
brilliant craftspeople.

ArtGlass Atelje (4, C5)
Slovene designer Tomaž
Miletič shows off the full
range of his skills with some
stunning pieces of glassware,
all beautifully displayed in
this classy studio.
☎ 426 31 04 🖥 www.
galerija-azbe.si ⊠ Dvorni
trg 2 ⏰ 10am-9pm Mon-
Fri, 10am-3pm Sat

Dom (4, D5)
A homewares souvenir shop –
the name means 'home'–
that sells everything from
wicker baskets to bottles of
slivovice, plus the usual
selection of bits and
bobs that say 'bought in
Ljubljana'.
☎ 241 83 00 ⊠ Mestni trg
24 ⏰ 9am-7pm Mon-Fri,
9am-1pm Sat

Galerija Zibka (4, C4)
It's a hotel boutique, but a
good one: the Lace Gallery
in the Hotel Slon is good
for lace and repro beehive
panels – perfect for that
1970s retro look that's all the
rage these days.
☎ 470 11 83 ⊠ Hotel Sion
Best Western, 4 Slovenska
cesta 34 ⏰ 10am-7pm
Mon-Fri, 10am-1pm Sat

Ljubljanček (4, D3)
Another hotel boutique,
Ljubljanček specialises in
decent-quality products and
souvenirs with distinctly
Ljubljančani motifs. Nothing
too adventurous.
☎ 308 19 40 ⊠ Grand
Hotel Union Executive,
Miklošičeva cesta 1 ⏰ 8am-
2pm & 3.30-7.30pm Mon-Fri,
8am-1pm Sat, 8am-noon Sun

Rustika (4, D5)
A huge arts and crafts shop
off the main yard of Ljubljana
Castle that does very good-
quality Idrija lace, fancy
glassware and woodcrafts
with prices to match.
☎ 031-383 247
⊠ Ljubljanska Grad
⏰ 10am-7pm Oct-May,
9.30am-8pm Jun-Sep

Skrina Galerija (4, C6)
This is the best shop – bar
none – for distinctly
Slovenian folk craft, albeit
aimed primarily at the tourist
market: Prekmurje black
pottery, Idrija lace, beehive
panels with folk motifs,
decorated heart-shaped
honey cakes, painted Easter
eggs, Rogaška glassware,
colourful bridal chests. Pay
cash and you pay less.
☎ 425 51 61 🖥 www.
skrina.si ⊠ Breg 8
⏰ 9am-7pm Mon-Fri,
9am-1pm Sat

JEWELLERY

Frey Willie (4, D5)
Distinctive enamel pieces and
accessories for both men and
women are the mainstay of
Viennese jeweller Friedrich
Willie, who founded the
original store in 1951 with
Michaela Frey. There are

Devilish Slovenian folk art

currently 34 branches throughout the world. ☎ 421 03 15 🖳 www. frey-willie.com ✉ Mestni trg 8 🕲 9am-7pm Mon-Fri, 9am-1pm Sat

BOOKS

Center Rokus (4, D5)
A well-stocked bookshop with a decent English-language section in the small room at the back – titles include a good selection of Lonely Planet guides! ☎ 244 38 80 🖳 www. rokus.com ✉ Mestni trg 6 🕲 10am-8pm Mon-Fri, 10am-5pm Sat

MUSIC

MCD (1, D2 & D4)
With two branches on the same street – one close to the bus station, the other opposite the Grand Hotel Union Executive – MCD is Ljubljana's best music shop, with informed, helpful staff. ☎ 425 17 06 🖳 www. mcd.si, in Slovenian ✉ Miklošičeva cesta 2 & Miklošičeva cesta 38 🕲 9am-8pm Mon-Fri, 9am-7pm Sat, 9am-1pm Sun

Musikalje (4, C6)
This atmospheric shop near the Križanke is the place for classical music and scores for all kinds of musicians. Even if you don't play, this place is special. ☎ 426 70 36 ✉ Trg Francoske Revolucije 6 🕲 9am-6pm Mon-Fri, 9am-1pm Sat

Spin Vinyl (4, D6)
A sizeable collection of old vinyl and CDs complements the newer stuff, which is a mix of alternative rock and dance music, both local and international. ☎ 251 10 18 🖳 www. spinvinyl.si ✉ Gallusovo nabrežje 13 🕲 10am-8pm Mon-Fri, 10am-6pm Sat-Sun

SPORTING GOODS

Outdoor pursuits – from walking to skiing – are a big deal in this city.

Annapurna (2, B1)
If you've forgotten your sleeping bag, ski poles, hiking boots or climbing gear, this shop in Krakovo can supply you with the same and more. ☎ 426 34 28 ✉ Krakovski nasip 4 🕲 9am-7pm Mon-Fri, 9am-1pm Sat

Lovec (4, C2)
The dream shop if it's just you against the wild. Lovec (Hunter) has everything you need if you're into ridin', fishin' and shootin'. Saddle up and be on your way. ☎ 231 73 87 ✉ Gosposvetska cesta 12 🕲 8am-7pm Mon-Fri, 8am-1pm Sat

WINE

Never tasted a Slovenian wine? Make up for it now; they've done some pretty tasty things with grapes.

Movia Vinoteka (4, D5)
An excellent wine bar where, with due ceremony and ritual, you can taste and buy your way through some award-winning Slovenian wines, including their own prized Movia vintages.

A LITTLE W(H)INE
Movia Vinoteka is undoubtedly the best place in town to feel like a wine connoisseur but it's pricier than everywhere else, so if you're not going to buy Movia's own excellent vintages, go elsewhere for the other producers.

☎ 425 54 48 ✉ Mestni trg 2 🕲 noon-midnight Mon-Sat

Vinoteka GR (3, C2)
This large wine cellar and restaurant has a selection of 800 wines, half of which are Slovenian. It's more affordable than some of the wine shops in the city centre. ☎ 431 50 15 ✉ Jurček Pavilion, Ljubljana Fairgrounds, Dunajska cesta 18 🕲 11am-11pm Mon-Fri

Vino Boutique (4, C3)
A smaller boutique with a choice selection of wines in all price ranges and a staff that are informative and helpful. ☎ 425 26 80 ✉ Slovenska cesta 38 🕲 10am-7pm Mon-Fri, 10am-1pm Sat

Eating

Eating is a pleasure in Ljubljana. Slovenian cuisine may not quite have – or deserve – the kudos reserved for what comes out of other European kitchens, but it manages very well with the limited range of dishes it does have. And in Ljubljana you can sample the best of them in a host of atmospheric restaurants spread throughout the city. The local palate has also developed a taste for food from beyond its own borders – nowadays you can eat anything from Serbian to sushi, although pizza and pastas from dear old next-door Italy are a perennial favourite.

MEAL COSTS

The pricing symbols used in this chapter indicate the cost of a two-course meal for one, with a drink. Bear in mind that for less than 1500SIT you probably won't get anything more than a snack and a drink rather than a sit-down meal.

€	under 1500SIT
€€	1500–3000SIT
€€€	3000–5000SIT
€€€€	over 5000SIT

OLD TOWN

Alamut Orient House (4, F4)
Iranian €€
Persian rugs and swords decorate this cosy little Iranian restaurant, whose 1400SIT lunch menus are popular with intellectuals and vegetarians. Subtle herbs and yogurt are used to masterful effect in the 1200SIT *polnjen malancan* (stuffed aubergine).
☎ 031 545 595
✉ Poljanska cesta 7
🕑 8am-10pm Mon-Sat
♿ V

Chez Eric (4, D5)
French €€€€
French cuisine at its exquisite best is what you'll get at this top-rated restaurant. The menu is small but carefully chosen – it simply means that the very *français* chef will stand over his creations and all (usually four meat and four fish) are as good as each other.
☎ 251 28 39 ✉ Mestni trg 3 🕑 noon-4pm & 7-11pm Mon-Sat

Gostilna Pri Pavli (4, D6)
Slovenian €€
A wonderful museum-like hangover from the socialist era, 'Paula's Place' is an attractive, country-style inn in an enviable location that has managed to retain its old-school prices. The Farmer's Feast (4200SIT) is a two-person smorgasbord of local tidbits, from grilled sausage to smoked meats and grilled veggies. Top notch.
☎ 425 92 75 ✉ Stari trg 1 🕑 6am-11pm ♿

Gostilna Sichuan (4, D6)
Chinese €€
If you're looking for Chinese food in Ljubljana, then you've probably taken a wrong turn somewhere. Of the handful in town, this is the oldest

Italy's just next door and pizza is a favourite

and probably the best, even though the standard menu is nothing too special. There are outdoor tables in summer.
☎ 251 93 37 ✉ Gornji trg 23 🕒 1pm-midnight Mon-Sat Ⓥ Some vegetarian dishes

Gostilna Vodnikov Hram (4, D4)
Slovenian €€
Not quite the tourist haven that is nearby Sokol (see p32), this inviting, vaulted pub attracts regulars from the market with its solid and affordable lunch specials, generally something meaty. There is, however, the odd vegetarian dish.
☎ 234 52 60 ✉ Vodnikov trg 2 🕒 8am-8pm Mon-Sat, food to 4pm Ⓥ Some vegetarian dishes

Julija (4, D5)
Italian €€
At Julija, risottos, pastas and other quasi-Italian dishes (salads, a couple of meat main courses) are served outside or in a pseudo-Delft tiled back room behind a café decorated with 1920s prints.
☎ 425 64 63 ✉ Stari trg 9 🕒 8am-10pm, café to midnight

Kavarna Zvezda (4, E2)
International €€
Ljubljana's most popular spot for choccy freaks and cake nuts, Zvezda does a roaring trade in desserts and other treats. We'd say three things about this place: it is exceedingly popular, the staff are a little tired and grumpy and the cakes are really, really good.
☎ 421 90 90 ✉ Kongresni trg 4 🕒 8am-9pm

Sokol (p32) is popular with locals and visitors alike

Luka Gourmet Lunch Café (4, D6)
American €€
Ljubljana's version of the New York downtown café is staffed by impossibly good-looking people serving a mildly Slovenian version of the ubiquitous brunch as well as other standard fare. It's a great spot for a late breakfast.
☎ 425 01 18 ✉ Stari trg 9 🕒 9am-11pm

Pri Sv Florijanu (4, D6)
Slovenian €€
This top-rate restaurant, housed in an old building with a stylishly modern interior, is famed for its creative nouveau-Slovenian cuisine. Venture downstairs

(open from 6pm) and you are atmospherically transported to North Africa for Moroccan food or a puff on a water pipe.
☎ 251 22 14 ✉ Gornji trg 20 🕒 noon-11pm Ⓥ Some vegetarian dishes

Ribca (4, D4)
Seafood Bar €
Just below the Plečnik Colonnade in Pogačarjev trg (accessible via the steps off Triple Bridge) is this basement seafood bar (Little Fish) serving tasty fried squid, sardines and herrings to hungry market-goers.
☎ 425 15 44 ✉ Adamič-Lundrovo nabrežje 1 🕒 8am-4pm Mon-Fri, 8am-2pm Sat

SERIOUS ABOUT SPUDS
Not only is it a damn fine restaurant, but Gostilna Pri Pavli is also the world HQ of the Society for the Recognition of Sautéed Potato and Onions as an Independent Dish. Finally a terrible and most egregious wrong is being redressed!

Try breakfast at the Luka Gourmet Lunch Café (p31)

Shanghai (4, F5)
Chinese €€
A surprisingly good Chinese restaurant that promises little when you're first handed the menu – complete with pictures for the total novice. The food, when it comes, is first-rate, even if it's standard Sichuan and Cantonese fare.
☎ 234 71 36 ✉ Poljanska cesta 14 ☾ 11am-11pm

Sokol (4, D5)
Slovenian €€
This faux-rustic *gostilna* (inn) is popular with everyone from market vendors taking their morning coffee to tour groups herded in for a bit of genuine grub, served on heavy tables by costumed waiters who stop just short of Disneyesque self-parody. Pizzas and vegetarian options are available if sausage and groats don't appeal.
☎ 439 68 55 ✉ Ciril Metodov trg 18 ☾ 10am-

11pm Ⓥ Some vegetarian dishes ♿

Taverna Tatjana (4, D6)
Seafood €€€
Looking like an old-world wooden-beamed cottage pub, this is actually a rather exclusive fish restaurant with a tiny, brilliant two-seat bar for your apéritif. As you leave, the view from the doorway is one of Ljubljana's most picturesque.
☎ 421 00 87 ✉ Gornji trg 38 ☾ 5pm-midnight

Zlata Ribica (4, D5)
International €€
Despite the ichthyological name, there's nary a finned creature on this riverfront restaurant's menu but lots of heavy Slovenian and central European dishes, including game. The menu has been recently expanded to include some Italian dishes, such as gnocchi with rocket.
☎ 426 94 90

🖳 www.zlataribica.com
✉ Cankarjevo nabrežje 5-7
☾ 8am-11pm

CENTER

Ajdovo Zrno (4, D4)
Vegetarian €
A recent arrival on the dining scene, Ajdovo Zrno – which means 'buckwheat grain' – serves soups, fried vegetables and lots of different salads. And terrific, freshly squeezed juices: rose-petal juice with lemon would make us want to live here forever.
☎ 041 690 478 🖳 www.satwa.si ✉ Trubarjeva cesta 7 ☾ 9am-8pm Mon-Fri, 11am-4pm Sat Ⓥ

Cantina Mexicana (4, C4)
Mexican €€
Smack in the heart of a busy, leafy laneway lined with bars and a couple of restaurants, this luridly colourful Mexican place has a fabulous terrace equipped with sofas and lanterns; perfect for a preprandial margarita to wash down that fajita. Prepare to wait as service is slow.
☎ 426 93 25 ✉ Knafljev prehod ☾ 11am-late ♿

Delikatesa Ljubljanski Dvor (4, C5)
Italian/International €
People queue at this gourmet shop, which offers all kinds of comestibles as well as huge, bargain pizza slices, salads and sold-by-weight braised veggies to take away or stand and eat.
☎ 426 93 27
✉ Gosposka ulica 2; takeaway service from

HOT HORSE

We're not kidding: one of the most popular fast foods in town is a huge burger bun stuffed with horse meat and relish, best enjoyed – or endured – at the end of a long night's drinking, which means that business is brisk around the 3am mark. The best places to try this questionable delicacy (as opposed to the kind of foal steak you'll find in some of the city's better restaurants) are:

• **Hot Horse** (4, A1; Tivoli Park; ⏱ 24hr) This popular stand is at the northern end of the park, near the National Museum of Contemporary History. It's busy during the day at weekends, but you'd really want to be keen on Hot Horse to traipse here late at night. Many are and do!

• **Hot Horse** (4, D4; Trubarjeva 31; ⏱ 24hr) Exactly what it says on the tin, this place exists to serve horse burgers and little else. The queues can be surprisingly long at night.

Kongresni trg 1
⏱ 9am-midnight Mon-Sat V

Figovec (4, C3)
Slovenian €€
This bustling and traditional eatery shows that there's more than one way to cook a horse and that pork trotters are a genuinely good main course. The less adventurous will find consolation in the seafood while vegetarians will just pull at their hair and despair.
☎ 426 50 00
✉ Gosposvetska cesta 1
⏱ 9am-midnight Mon-Sat, noon-5pm Sun

Gostilna As (4, C4)
Seafood €€€€
The place to go for that special blow-out meal, the 'Ace Inn' is Ljubljana's most formal restaurant — you'll only feel comfortable if you dress the part — and a pretty

good place to eat seafood and a handful of Slovene classics. The attached terrace bistro is cheaper, more relaxed and a good place for pizza, pastas and salad.
☎ 425 88 22
✉ Knafljev prehod 5a; also enter from Čopova ulica 5a or Slovenska cesta 30 ⏱ noon-midnight

JB (4, D2)
Mediterranean €€€€
Old-world charm, a top-notch wine list and a catch-all, hybrid Slovenian-Mediterranean-French menu have made this restaurant one of the most popular in town for a fancy meal. If you can't get a table at Gostilna As or Smrekarjev Hram, this is a good third choice.
☎ 474 72 19
✉ Miklošičeva cesta 17
⏱ 11am-midnight Mon-Fri, 6pm-midnight Sat

Joe Pena's Cantina y Bar (4, C3)
Mexican €€
Lazily whirring ceiling fans, earth-tone walls and wooden floors create plenty of atmosphere at Joe Pena's, Ljubljana's best, mood-lit Mexican restaurant. Burritos, fajitas and other bean-rich classics are the stars of the show.
☎ 421 50 00 ✉ Cankarjeva cesta 6 ⏱ 10am-1am Mon-Sat, noon-midnight Sun

Operna Klet (4, B4)
Seafood €€€
This old-style restaurant near the Opera (the name means 'opera cellar') concentrates on seafood and has a pleasant inner courtyard for al fresco dining in the warmer months. Enter from Tomšičeva ulica.
☎ 252 70 03
✉ Župančičeva ulica 2
⏱ 11am-11pm

Pizzerija Foculus (4, B6)
Pizza €€
Fifty different kinds of pizza make for a bewildering choice at this busy, noisy

Slovenian fast food at Tomato (p34)

The elegant vaulted dining room of Pri Vitezu

place that probably serves the best version of the Italian pie in town — and considering pizza's popularity, that's really saying something.

☎ 251 56 43 🖥 www.foculus.com
✉ Gregorčičeva ulica 3
🕐 10am-midnight Mon-Fri, 11am-midnight Sat & Sun ⚓

Pri Vitezu (4, C6)
Seafood €€€€
Located directly on the left bank of the Ljubljanica, 'At the Knight' is the place for a special meal (Mediterranean-style and Adriatic fish dishes), whether in the vaulted cellar dining rooms or the adjoining wine bar.

☎ 426 60 58 ✉ Breg 18-20 🕐 noon-midnight Mon-Sat

Šestica (4, C3)
Slovenian €€
Devoted patrons have been tucking into dishes like *goveji golaž* (beef goulash) and *svinjska pečenka* (roast pork) since 1776, which makes this the perfect destination for today's curious tourist. The *prekmurska gibanica* — a layered cake filled with poppy seeds, apples, cheese, walnuts, and raisins topped with warm melted chocolate — is divine.

☎ 242 08 55 ✉ Slovenska cesta 40 🕐 10am-11pm Mon-Fri, noon-11pm Sat

Smrekarjev Hram (4, C4)
International €€€€
'Smrekar's House', an art nouveau jewel run by the Grand Hotel Union, is named after artist and illustrator Hinko Smrekar (1883–1942), famed for his 'pan-Slavic' playing cards. It has always been considered the poshest international restaurant in Ljubljana. It is, but you can eat better elsewhere.

☎ 308 12 70 ✉ Nazorjeva ulica 2 🕐 noon-11pm Mon-Fri 🅥

Sushimama (4, C4)
Japanese €€€
Straight lines and dark wood set the tone for the city's best — ok, only — Japanese restaurant, where the sushi chef dices and slices before your eyes (if they should strain towards the open kitchen) while the suitably ice-cold waiting staff serve his work with expert ease. Not especially friendly, but very good.

☎ 070-72 72 72 ✉ Wolfova ulica 12 🕐 11am-11pm Mon-Sat

Tomato (4, B4)
Fast Food €
Decent sandwiches, healthy salads and well-made burgers are the mainstay of this enormously popular fast-food joint in the heart of Center. The sandwich options alone will keep you coming back for more, while the freshly made juices are sensational.

☎ 252 75 55 ✉ Šubičeva

BUREK: THE GREASY LOWDOWN

Originally introduced by the Turks as *börek*, *burek* – the favourite post-booze, pre-sleep snack of all Ljubljana – is filo pastry usually stuffed with ground beef. Other variations include cheese *burek* (for vegetarians) or even pizza *burek* (for Italophiles). To look at, it's a greasy, delicious mess and there's no elegant way to eat it: you just stuff it into your mouth and use as many napkins as you can to wipe your hands. There are a bunch of *burek* stands around the city centre, but we recommend the following (if only for convenience's sake!)

• **Nobel Burek** (4, D2; Miklošičeva cesta 30; burek 450SIT; ☽ 24hr) Not quite noble, nor should it win any kind of international award, but when you're hungry, it really hits the spot.

ulica 1 ☽ 7am-10pm Mon-Fri, 8am-4pm Sat

Unionska Klet (4, D3)
Slovenian/International €€€
This atmospheric cellar restaurant is the flagship of the Grand Hotel Union Executive (p44). The largely Slovenian cuisine is the preferred choice but there is an excellent selection of more familiar international dishes to suit the less adventurous palates of the largely business clientele.
☎ 308 19 68
✉ Miklošičeva cesta 1
☽ noon-11pm

KRAKOVO & TRNOVO

Breskvar (3, C6)
Slovenian €€€
This cosy *gostilna* (inn) in Trnovo is an absolute find, a little bit of rustic delight in the middle of Ljubljana. It serves some of the finest home-cooking in town, and the shady garden is a delight

when the warmer months roll around.
☎ 283 88 33 ✉ Cesta na Loko 28 ☽ noon-10pm Mon-Fri, noon-5pm Sun

Harambaša (2, B2)
Bosnian €€
One of Ljubljana's best-loved restaurants is this traditional Bosnian eatery in the heart of Krakovo, where *čevapčiči*

(a kind of meatball, see p36) is served with *kaymak* cheese in traditional Balkan bread. For afters, Turkish coffee comes with a cigarette. Absolutely top class.
☎ 041-675 155 ✉ Vrtna ulica 8 ☽ 10am-10pm Mon-Fri, noon-10pm Sat, noon-6pm Sun

Manna (2, B2)
International €€€
Written across the door is 'Božanske jedi na zemlji' – 'heavenly food on earth'. That's a bit of a stretch, but this stylish eatery along the canal is pretty nice. Try the rocket dumplings with scampi and saffron.
☎ 283 52 94 ✉ Eipprova ulica 1A ☽ noon-midnight Mon-Fri, noon-10pm Sat

Pri Škofu (2, A2)
Slovenian €€
The rustic cuisine 'At the Bishop's' isn't to everyone's taste, but if you like the carefully prepared local dishes served at

Sweet treats at Pri Vitezu (opposite)

this tiny, unpretentious restaurant – it's as if you're being fed by someone's Slovenian grandmother who really can cook – then you'll absolutely love it and you'll just keep coming back for more.

☎ 426 45 08 ✉ Rena ulica 8 🕑 8am-midnight Mon-Fri, noon-midnight Sat & Sun 🚹

Trta (2, C2)
Pizza €€

If you absolutely must satisfy that craving for pizza, then 'Grapevine', a canalside pizzeria on the right bank opposite Trnovo, is the place to go. There's no nicer spot to enjoy that slice than by the water's edge.

☎ 426 50 66
✉ Grudnovo nabrežje 21
🕑 11am-10.30pm Mon-Fri, noon-10.30pm Sat

WORTH A TRIP

Casa del Papa (3, A1)
Spanish/Caribbean €€

'Papa' refers to Ernest Hemingway, and his 'house' is decorated in a hotchpotch of styles related to the American author's life and travels: Spanish here, Cuban there, African somewhere over there. Somehow it all works, and the place remains popular with well-heeled Ljubljančani.

☎ 434 31 58
✉ Celovška cesta 54
🕑 noon-1am V

Gostilna Rožnik (3, A3)
Slovenian €€

This hilltop restaurant is an insider favourite, especially at weekends when locals crowd the outdoor seating

for honest-to-goodness Slovene staples such as *pečenica z zeljen* (sausage with cabbage) and *jota* (a buckwheat, meat and cabbage stew) to be enjoyed with some good Union beer and a terrific view of the city below and the surrounding greenery of Park Tivoli.

☎ 251 34 29 🖥 www. gostilna-roznik.com ✉ Cankarjev vrh 1 🕑 10am-9pm May-Sep, 10am-7pm Oct-Apr 🚹

Pod Rožnikom (3, A3)
Serbian €€€

The name means 'under Mt Rožnik' but most refer to it simply as 'Čad'. It serves southern Slavic-style grills such as *pleskavica* (spicy meat patties) with *avar* (roasted red peppers, tomatoes and aubergine cooked into a purée) and – for the truly adventurous – a tasty *biftek žrebičov* (foal steak).

☎ 251 34 46 ✉ Cesta na Rožnik 18 🕑 10am-11pm Mon-Fri, 11am-11pm Sat & Sun

Pri Katrci (3, A4)
Slovenian €€€

In the heart of Ljubljana's fanciest residential neighbourhood is this traditional *gostilna* (inn) that serves up hearty Slovenian fare, including some delicious homemade bread. They also do a wide selection of pizzas, just to cover all the bases. It's only worth seeking out if you're already in the neighbourhood.

☎ 422 88 40 🖥 www. katrca.8k.com ✉ Cesta I 26a, Rožna Dolina 🕑 8am-midnight P

Vegedrom (3, B1)
Vegetarian €-€€

Ljubljana's first truly vegetarian restaurant serves meat- and egg-free dishes, including tasty veggie platters for two (4200–5000SIT) and other good-for-you delights. There's a salad bar for that healthy takeaway. It's at the northeastern edge of Park Tivoli.

☎ 519 39 01 ✉ Vodnikova cesta 35 🕑 9am-10pm Mon-Fri, noon-10pm Sat V

Čevapčiči – another typical Ljubljana dish

Entertainment

Few European cities of comparable size to Ljubljana offer such a dizzying array of drinking options, whether your poison is beer and spirits or tea and coffee. The line between café and bar is somewhat blurred, as you can get a beer in most cafés and tea in most bars. And they come in all shapes – from the old-style boozer to the kind of place vying for a centrefold spread in a style magazine.

But it's not all about liquids. Ljubljana enjoys a rich cultural and social life, from the highest of highbrow pursuits to grungy alternative expression. *Where to? In Ljubljana* and *Ljubljana Calling* (www.ljubljana-calling.com) list cultural events, sports and nightlife options. Glossy *Ljubljana Life* (www.ljubljanalife.com) has some refreshingly frank reviews. All three magazines are free from TICs, hotels and some restaurants.

BARS & PUBS

Ljubljana's lovely young things hang out at Fraga (p38)

As Lounge (4, C4)
In 2005 Slovenia's first-ever reality TV show was filmed here, based on the goings-on of a bunch of beautiful people 'working' in this terribly cool disco-bar. Regular queues at weekends reveal that its clientele are mostly the pretty and impressionable young things of Ljubljana.
☎ 425 88 22 ✉ beneath Gostilna As (p33), Knafljev prehod 5a € free before 11pm ⏰ 9am-3am

Bar Minimal (4, D5)
Paler than white, cooler than frost, Bar Minimal is getting a tad worn around its brilliant edges, but it's a slice of designer style in the Old Town. Great for a coffee during the day and the spot to be seen with a glass in hand in the evening.
☎ 426 01 38 ✉ Mestni trg 4 ⏰ 8am-1am

BiKoFe (4, C5)
A favourite with the hipster crowd, this small, smoky bar has mosaic tables, student art on the walls, soul and jazz on the stereo and a giant water pipe *(vodna pipa)* on the menu for that long, lingering smoke (850SIT). Cool as hell but not a bit pretentious.
✉ Gosposka 7 ⏰ 5pm-2am Tue-Sun

Čarli (4, D4)
The city centre's last remaining socialist-style boozer is renowned for its convivial, friendly atmosphere – its regulars (a good mix of young and old) treat it like a second home.

BEST BOOZERS
With so many options to choose from, here's a top five to help you make that choice:
- **BiKoFe** Drink and smoke in artistic company
- **Bar Minimal** Frosty white for style
- **Čarli** For that old-style drink
- **Kavarna Pločnik** You'll end up here anyway…
- **Sax Pub** Live jazz and nice people

The cat drags them in at Maček

Chess fiends come here on Sundays to play against each other. A slice of pre-independence Ljubljana.
☎ 232 81 83
✉ Petkovškovo nabrežje 21
🕐 9am-3am

Druga Pomoč (3, E3)
'Second Aid' – across the road from the local ER – is the quintessential dive bar, a friendly place that is the perfect pitstop on the way to a Metelkova club (p40) or the best place to while away an evening. A pleasant little courtyard makes summer drinking that bit more fun.
☎ 431 32 77
✉ Šmartinska cesta 3
🕐 6pm-3am

Cutty Sark Pub (4, C4)
The nautical name and theme are but a beard; this is Ljubljana's version of a traditional English pub, with a little bit of Irish thrown in for good measure. The perfect spot to get drunk with the increasing numbers of British hen and stag parties flying in for the weekend.
☎ 425 14 77 ✉ Knafljev prehod 1 🕐 9am-1am Mon-Sat, 2pm-1am Sun

Fraga (4, D5)
Seriously happening Fraga attracts the impossibly cool and improbably young things of Ljubljana during the day with its trendy mix of good coffee and even better art gallery. The average age creeps up in the evening but it's still a stylin' place.

☎ 426 90 05 ✉ Mestni trg 15 🕐 9am-1am Mon-Sat

Kavarna Pločnik (4, C4)
The Pavement Café on the southern side of Prešernov trg is one of the most popular places for a drink if you just want to sit outside and watch the passing parade. You'll probably bump into half the people you've met along the way in Slovenia here. There's live music and puppet shows from late June to August.
✉ Prešernov trg 1 🕐 7am-1am Apr-Oct

Maček (4, C5)
Popular, usually packed and utterly devoid of personality, the 'Cat' draws the tourist crowds because…we're not really sure. It's in a great location on the right bank of the Ljubljanica and is a cross between a traditional Slovenian bar and an English pub. Reasons enough? No.
☎ 425 37 91 ✉ Krojaška ulica 5 🕐 9am-1am

Sax Pub (2, B2)
Straight out of East Village, this smoky dive bar is one of the best bars in town – if you can find a spot to stand in! The walls are plastered with

THE CLASH OF THE BEERS
Slovenia's most popular beers are the Ljubljana-brewed Union, easily recognised by its distinctive red label, and the green-labelled Laško, brewed in the town of the same name in the northeastern Štajerska region. Which is the best? In Ljubljana they'll obviously fly the flag for Union, but why is it then that a popular Slovenian saying states that 'you drink Laško, you piss Union'? Ehm, I'll take a Laško please.

photos of sax greats Rashaan Roland Kirk, John Coltrane and Charlie Parker.
☎ 283 90 09 ✉ Eipprova ulica 7 ⏱ 10am-1am Tue-Sun

CAFÉS & TEAHOUSES

Abecedarium Café (4, D5)
Ensconced in the oldest house (1528) in Ljubljana and one-time residence of the writer Primož Trubar is this pleasant café, a quiet and comfy place to while away an afternoon and nurse a glass of wine or a cup of coffee.
☎ 426 95 14 ✉ Ribji trg 2 ⏱ 7am-1am ♿

Café Antico (4, D6)
A handsome old-style café with frescoed ceilings and antique furniture, the appositely named Café Antico is the perfect place for a quiet tête-à-tête over a glass of Slovenian wine, a piping hot coffee or a drenched tiramisú – booze-in-a-bun.

☎ 425 13 39 ✉ Stari trg 17 ⏱ 7am-midnight Sun-Thu, 7am-1am Fri & Sat ♿

Café Galerija (4, D5)
Tucked almost secretly away at the back of a small modern art gallery is this stylish arabesque café with inlaid brass tables, coloured glass and cosy nooks. DJs play progressive house from 10pm every night except Sunday.
☎ 426 03 27 ✉ Mestni trg 5 ⏱ 9am-1am Mon-Sat, 9am-10pm Sun

Caffè Galerija Dvorni Trg (4, C5)
The art on the walls is so-so, which makes the café the best bit about this riverside gallery, which some claim has the best coffee in town. Not quite, but close, and good enough to keep us coming back for more.
☎ 426 40 97 ✉ Dvorni trg 2 ⏱ 8am-1am Mon-Sat

Čajna Hiša (4, D5)
The Teahouse is an exquisite art nouveau café with a

small streetside terrace, but the real treat is indoors, where you can drink your tea (or coffee) before slipping in to the attached shop. Here you can buy dozens of different kinds of teas and a host of lovely pots to serve them in.
☎ 425 52 13 ✉ Stari trg 3 ⏱ 9am-11pm Mon-Fri, 9am-3pm & 6-11pm Sat ♿

Global (4, C4)
On the 6th floor of the Nana department store (and accessed via an elevator on Slovenska cesta) this large, modern café-bar has the best views in town from the balcony, but it's definitely more of a nighttime destination, when the place turns into a throbbing nightclub (p41).
☎ 426 90 17 🖥 www.global.si ✉ Tomšičeva ulica 2 ⏱ 8am-5am Tue-Sat, 8am-9pm Mon

KavaČaj (4, C2)
This traditional café slightly off the beaten path is a real

Watch the world go by at Kavarna Pločnik (opposite)

gem, a virtual hangover from another era and one of the best places in town to sample a wide array of fruit teas and coffees.

☎ 433 82 33 ✉ Kersnikova ulica 1 🕑 7.30am-10pm Mon-Thu, 7.30am-9pm Fri, 9am-2pm Sun ♿

Slaščičarna Pri Vodnjaku (4, D6)

For all kinds of chocolate of the ice cream and drinking kind, the 'Sweet House by the Fountain' will surely satisfy – there are 32 different flavours on the menu, courtesy of those Italian masters at Antica Cioccolateria. Non-choccy heads are catered for too (but what's wrong with you?).

☎ 425 07 12 ✉ Stari trg 30 🕑 8am-midnight ♿

Tramvaj Ekspres (3, B4)

Although trams similar to these two plied the streets of Ljubljana until 1958, these imports from Prague were not among them. Still, it's worth a visit for the novelty of sipping your espresso in a vintage tramcar.

☎ 425 47 82 ✉ Trg Mladinskih Delovnih Brigad 10 🕑 10am-9pm Mon-Fri Jun-Sep, 10am-5pm Mon-Fri Oct-May ♿

NIGHTCLUBS

As Lounge (4, C4)

Before 11pm, this is just another of Ljubljana's trendy new bars; come the witching hour, the queues get longer, the bouncers get stricter, the music gets louder and the dance floor fills to capacity with short-skirted gals and guys in immaculately pressed shirts. The music is straight out of a 'Now!' collection.

☎ 425 88 22 🖥 www.gostilnaas.si, in Slovenian until 1958, these ✉ beneath Gostilna As, Knafljev prehod 5a € 600-1000SIT 🕑 9am-3am

Bachus Center (4, C4)

This expansive underground complex is a contender for top club in town. It includes a daytime café, a restaurant and a pretty decent dance club, which won't challenge the musical extremes but certainly knows how to keep the young punters very happy. The dance club is open Thursday to Saturday.

☎ 241 82 44 🖥 www.bachus-center.com, in Slovenian ✉ Kongresni trg € 600-1500SIT 🕑 8am-1am Mon-Wed, 8am-4am Thu-Sat, 6pm-4am holidays

Discoteka Fun Factory (3, off B6)

Ljubljana's biggest nightclub has all the essentials of a big-time dance venue – top name visiting DJs on the

METELKOVA MADNESS

Half a dozen wonderfully idiosyncratic venues make up the two-courtyard block that is **Metelkova** (www.metelkova.org). Behind the mostly unmarked doors, the venues really come to life Thursday to Saturday from late – nothing much goes on before 11pm or midnight. Entering from Masarykova cesta, to the right is **Gala Hala** (3, D3; www.ljudmila.org/kapa/program, in Slovenian) with live bands and club nights. Easy to miss in the first building to the left are **Club Tiffany** (3, D3; www.ljudmila.org/siqrd/tiffany, in Slovenian), a gay café-club; and the predominantly lesbian **Monokel** (3, E3; www.ljudmila.org/lesbo/monokel, in Slovenian). Beyond the first courtyard, well-hidden **Klub Gromka** (3, E3; www.metelkova.org/gromka, in Slovenian) – beneath the bodyless heads – puts on a mixed programme of folk, improv and almost anything else. Cover charges and midweek openings are rare but erratic for all Metelkova venues.

HAPPY DECEMBER!

Christmas month in Ljubljana is officially known as *Veseli December* (Happy December), a time of…erm… celebration. The whole town drinks more than usual, eats more than its fill and generally gets a little crazy until the dawn of the New Year. Needless to say, it's impossible to get any real work done during that time, but no one seems to mind. *Veseli December!*

main floor, great resident in the lounge, a handful of bars and a chillout room. It's 3km south of the city centre.
☎ 428 96 90 🖳 www.discoteka-funfactory.com ✉ Industrija cona Rudnik, Jurčkova 224 € 1500-2500SIT ☯ 9pm-4am Wed-Sat 🚌 19 to Rudnik, direction Livada

Global (4, C4)

It's one of the most popular nightclubs in town – judging from the seemingly endless queue at the elevator doors on Slovenska cesta – and what awaits you on the sixth floor is the same mix of house music and other beats that you'd get in every other commercially minded club in Europe. The young and the beautiful just can't get enough of it.
☎ 426 90 17 🖳 www.global.si ✉ Tomšičeva ulica 2 € free before midnight, 1000SIT after ☯ 8am-5am Tue-Sat, 8am-9pm Mon

K4 (4, C2)

Two stark dance floors beneath the student organisation Roza Klub (p55) – you enter the basement club from the rear – feature techno and house on Friday and Saturday, with other styles of music weeknights (rap, folk, even some

nu jazz), and a popular gay-and-lesbian night on Sunday.
☎ 431 70 10 🖳 www.klubk4.org ✉ Kersnikova ulica 4 € 500-1500SIT ☯ 10pm-4am

LIVE MUSIC

Jazz Club Gajo (4, B4)

The premier venue for live jazz is this convivial club just up from the parliament building. Monday nights are jam nights open to anybody who can play, while other nights feature a wide array of live performance of both local and international talent.
☎ 425 32 06 🖳 www.jazzclubgajo.com ✉ Beethovnova 8 € free-1000SIT ☯ 11am-2am Mon-Fri, 7pm-midnight Sat & Sun

The sound of sax at Jazz Club Gajo

Orto Bar (3, E3)

Popular for late-night drinking and dancing with occasional live music (from rock and punk to blues and hip hop); and red padded walls, whirring steel propeller fans and a taste for Joy Division. It's just five minutes' walk from Metelkova.

☎ 232 16 74
✉ Graboličeva ulica 1
€ free ☼ 8am-4am Sun-Thu, 6pm-5am Fri & Sat

Sax Pub (2, B2)

You won't find a more atmospheric – or smoky – venue to hear live jazz than this canalside dive bar in Trnovo. Musicians work their jazzy vibes from the cramped corner while the ultra-appreciative audience crams into the rest of the small space to listen, drink and nod their heads in approval.

☎ 283 90 09 ✉ Eipprova ulica 7 € free ☼ 10am-1am Tue-Sun

THEATRE & CLASSICAL MUSIC

Cankarjev Dom (4, A5)

This extraordinary cultural and performance complex is made up of around a dozen venues offering a remarkable smorgasbord of performance arts. The main venue alone hosts about 1000 events a year.

☎ 241 73 00 ☐ www.cd-cc.si ✉ venue: Prešernova cesta 10; ticket office: basement of Maximarket, Trg Republike (4, B5) ☼ 11am-1pm & 3-8pm Mon-Fri, 11am-1pm Sat, & 1hr before performances

Filharmonija (4, C5)

Home to the Slovenian Philharmonic Orchestra, the small but atmospheric Philharmonic Hall stages concerts and hosts performances of the Slovenian Chamber Choir (Slovenski Komorni Zbor), which was founded in 1991. The attractive late 19th-century building was sympathetically renovated in 2001. Buy tickets from the ticket office at Cankarjev Dom (see left).

☎ 241 08 00 ☐ www.filharmonija.si ✉ Kongresni trg 10

Križanke (4, C6)

The outdoor theatre at this sprawling 18th-century monastery is the primary host of the events of the Ljubljana Summer Festival (see Special Events box opposite). The Križanke's Knights Hall (Viteška Dvorana) is the venue for chamber concerts and plays.

☎ 252 65 44 ☐ www.festival-lj.si ✉ Trg francoske revolucije 1-2. Box office ☎ 241 60 26 ☼ 10am-1.30pm & 4-8pm Mon-Fri, 10am-1pm Sat & 1hr before performances.

NOVI PROGRAM 05/06

Slovenska filharmonija

The Slovenian Philharmonic presents a colourful classical programme

Slovenian National Opera & Ballet Theatre (4, B4)

The neo-Renaissance 1882 Slovensko Narodno Gledališče Opera in Balet theatre stages both opera and ballet of the highest quality, a testament to the careful attention paid to the classical arts in Ljubljana.

☎ 241 17 40 🖳 www.operainbalet-lj.si
✉ Župančičeva ulica 1
Box office ☎ 241 17 64
🕑 1-5pm Mon-Fri, 11am-1pm Sat & 1hr before performances.

CINEMAS

Slovenska Kinoteka (4, D2)

The most imaginative programme in town, including rare, old and cult movies, in an art deco mansion. If the linguistic challenges of following a Slovene soundtrack are getting you down, slope off for a drink in the attached atmospheric, movie-themed Marilyn Caffe (big beers 380SIT).

☎ 613 13 91 🖳 www.kinoteka.si, in Slovene
✉ Miloševičeva cesta 28
€ 1400SIT

Kolosej (3, off F1)

A run-of-the-mill, 12-screen multiplex in the BTC City shopping centre northeast of Center. It shows the usual first-run films about six months after their general release in the US and Britain.

☎ 520 55 00 🖳 www.kolosej.si, in Slovene
✉ Šmartinska cesta 152
🚌 2, 7, 17 to BTC City

SPECIAL EVENTS

JUNE

Druga Godba (Other Music; www.drugagodba.si) A festival of alternative and world music; takes place in the Križanke in early June.

International Biennial of Graphic Arts (www.mglc-lj.si) At the International Centre of Graphic Arts in Park Tivoli, the Modern Art Museum and several other venues. Continues into September.

Ljubljana Jazz Festival (www.cd-cc.si) At the Križanke in late June; has been taking place for 45 years.

Vino Ljubljana (Ljubljanski Sejem; Ljubljana Fairgrounds, Dunajska cesta 10) An international wine fair held in early June north of the train station.

JULY

Ljubljana Summer Festival (www.festiva-lj.si) The number-one event on Ljubljana's social calendar, a summer celebration of music, opera, dance and street theatre held in venues throughout the city, but principally in the open-air theatre at the Križanke (opposite). Continues until late August.

Summer in the Old Town Ljubljana is at its most vibrant in July and August during the so-called Summer in the Old Town season when there are four or five free cultural events a week in the city's historic squares, courtyards and bridges. Contact the tourist office for more information.

Trnfest (www.kud-fp.si) An international festival of alternative arts and culture organised by KUD France Prešeren; takes place in Trnovo from late July through into August.

AUGUST

Young Lions (Mladi Levi; bunker@siol.net) A 10-day festival of theatre and dance held in late August.

OCTOBER

City of Women (www.cityofwomen.org) In venues throughout Ljubljana; showcases all forms of artistic expression by women.

Ljubljana Marathon (www.slo-timing.com) Starts and ends in Kongresni trg; held on the last Saturday in October.

Sleeping

There isn't an especially good choice of accommodation in Ljubljana. You can pretty much count the better options on the fingers of one hand, while the rest are a decent mix of midrange hangovers from another era, student and private accommodation and small business hotels where character is sacrificed in favour of comfort.

However, as the city gains a firmer foothold on the tourist map, things are changing. New hotels and hostels are being built and handsome old properties are being converted into elegant hotels. You may not have a lot of choice just yet, but it's going to get better.

DELUXE

Domina Grand Media Hotel & Casino (4, off D1)

Ljubljana goes high-end and high-tech with this elegant new hotel on the outskirts of the city. An all-pervasive Japanese influence makes for thoroughly modern rooms equipped with fully integrated flat-screen or – in the better rooms – plasma-screen TVs, VOIP phones (which means all landline calls are free) and other electronic gadgetry.
☎ 588 25 00 ☐ www.dominagmljubljana.com ✉ Dunajska cesta 154 ♿ 🚌 5, 8 to ring road

Grand Hotel Union Executive (4, D3)

The capital's star address is this art nouveau classic that celebrated its 100th birthday in 2005. The huge rooms are elegantly decorated with handsome cherrywood furniture, while the views from the eighth- and ninth-floor rooms in the newer wing (1966) are fantastic. ISDN lines are in every room; some have WiFi internet connection.
☎ 308 12 70 ☐ www.gh-union.si ✉ Miklošičeva cesta 1 ♿ 🍴 Unionska Klet, Smrekarjev Hram (p34)

Hotel Lev (4, B2)

It's certainly luxurious, but we think there's something a little nondescript about this deluxe 173-room hotel. The rooms are perfectly fine, the furnishings pleasant enough (the bathrooms are tiny) but the whole package just

Art nouveau splendour at the Grand Hotel Union Executive

doesn't add up to the high-end prices.

☎ 433 21 55 🖵 www.hotel-lev.si ✉ Vošnjakova ulica 1

TOP END

Cityhotel Turist (4, D3)
Beyond the Eastern-Bloc-in-the-1970s lobby is quite a smart international hotel that was given a thorough once-over in 2002. The standard doubles are a little on the smallish side, but all the singles have queen-sized beds and there is WiFi internet connection throughout the building.

☎ 234 91 30 🖵 www.hotelturist.si ✉ Dalmatinova ulica 15 ♿

Grand Hotel Union Business (4, D3)
A recent renovation of the business-oriented branch of the Grand Hotel Union has resulted in rooms that look more or less like the ones in the Executive (minus the art nouveau touches). Although not as expensive as its posher sister next door, the difference is negligible.

☎ 308 11 70 🖵 www.gh-union.si ✉ Miklošičeva cesta 3 ♿ ✗ Unionska Klet, Smrekarjev Hram (p34)

Grand Hotel Union Garni (4, D2)
The latest addition to the Union empire is the former Hotel Astral, a warm and friendly socialist-style hotel that caters predominantly for business customers midweek and leisure travellers at weekends. Long, monotonous corridors give way to attractive, good-sized and pleasantly furnished rooms. A new name for the hotel is planned for 2006.

☎ 308 43 01 🖵 www.gh-union.si ✉ Miklošičeva cesta 9 ♿

Hotel Mons (3, off A5)
A brand new, ultra-stylish four-star hotel with comfortable, high-tech rooms and a colourful designer look throughout the entire glassed-in building. It may be exactly what the tourist doctor ordered, but it's just that little bit too far out of town to cater for the non-business crowd. However, there is a free shuttle bus service to Kongresni trg.

☎ 470 27 00 🖵 www.hotel.mons.si ✉ Pot za Brdom 55 ♿ 🚌 1, 6 to Brdo

Smart international style at the Cityhotel Turist

Hotel Slon Best Western (4, C4)
Elegant in an Eastern Bloc kind of way, the 171-room 'Hotel Elephant' has joined the Best Western family, who will undoubtedly continue to fix and fiddle with it so that it meets the exacting needs of the contemporary business travellers. The corner suites all have whirlpool baths.

☎ 470 11 00 🖵 www.hotelslon.com ✉ Slovenska cesta 34

MIDRANGE

Hotel Emonec (4, C4)
The décor is coldly modern but everything is gleamingly clean and you can't beat the central location. TVs and internet access in every room are unusual niceties for the price, making this hotel excellent value for money.

☎ 200 15 20 🖵 www.hotel-emonec.com ✉ Wolfova ulica 12 ♿

APARTMENT RENTAL
Private, fully furnished and serviced apartments are a popular option for both short- and long-term visitors to Ljubljana. The best agency in the business is:
• **Tour As** (4, D3; ☎ 434 26 60; www.apartmaji.si; Mala ulica 8; ♿) A well-run business with 35 one- to three-bedroom apartments spread about the city centre and the near suburbs. Prices range from €35–118 per day.

Hotel Park (4, F3)

This tower-block hangover from socialist Yugoslavia in a handily convenient if rather uninviting area is central Ljubljana's best-value midrange choice. The rooms are a little basic but pleasant nonetheless. We love the old-style lifts: one for even-numbered floors, another for odd-numbered ones. Cheaper rooms have en-suite toilet but share showers.
☎ 300 25 00 ☐ www.hotelpark.si ✉ Tabor 9 ♿

M Hotel (3, off F1)

About 2km northwest of Center and not much to look at from outside, but this is a very good hotel with 154 comfortable rooms, all with the usual mod-cons includings ISDN lines and cable TV. Park Tivoli is just around the corner.
☎ 513 70 00 ☐ www.m-hotel.si ✉ Derčeva ulica 4 ☐ 1, 5, 8, 15 to Kino Šiška stop ♿ ♿ good (2 rooms designed for wheelchair access)

Pri Mraku (4, B6)

Above the good but dowdy-looking restaurant is this warm and friendly guesthouse with a bunch of slightly cramped rooms squeezed in on top of each other. The fit may be a little tight but it's comfortable and the location is excellent.
☎ 433 40 49 ☐ www.daj-dam.si/ang/Mrak/mrakmain.htm ✉ Rimska cesta 4

BUDGET

Alibi Hostel (4, C5)

Once the location of the British Consulate, the newest – and best-positioned – hostel in town is still very much a work in progress, but by the time you read this they should have everything up and running. They manage two other properties: one (Alibi K5) a few doors away, the other in the near suburb of Bežigrad.
☎ 031 363 666 ☐ www.alibi.si ✉ Cankarjevo Nabrežje 27

BIT Center Hotel (3, F4)

About 2 km east of the Old Town is this great-value hotel, although its location is off-putting if you want to be close to the action. Its 37 rooms are spartan but bright and comfortable, there's a good buffet breakfast and guests can use the hotel's sports centre, which includes a pool, gym, squash and badminton courts.
☎ 548 00 55 ☐ www.bit-center.net ✉ Litijska 57 ♿ ☐ 9, 13 to Emona stop

Celica Hostel (3, D3)

The best hostel in the world? It's certainly a contender: the cells in this former military prison have been redesigned by different architects in different styles – from Finnish to traditional Slovenian – and the results are so wonderful that there are guided tours every day at 2pm. Absolutely brilliant.
☎ 230 97 00 ☐ www.hostelcelica.com ✉ Metelkova ulica 8 ♿

Some hotels supply earplugs – just in case

About Ljubljana

HISTORY
Celts & Romans
Bronze Age marsh dwellers living in huts on stilts aren't in the business of civilisation-building, and it was no different here. It took the arrival of the Illyrians and, in the 4th century BC, the Celts, to make a significant mark on the banks of the Ljubljanica. But it was the militaristic and organised Romans who made a real difference. In the first century BC they built a military camp here and called it Emona – by the time of Christ it was a thriving town of 5000 inhabitants.

The Habsburgs
Throughout the Middle Ages, nothing much happened to Ljubljana that didn't happen to most other towns. This little burg changed hands a few times until 1335, when the Habsburgs took control. They named it Laibach and, with one brief interlude in the 19th century, didn't relinquish it until 1918, at the end of WWI.

Under Habsburg rule Ljubljana flourished as a trading centre. It fought off the Turks in the 15th century, and following a devastating earthquake in 1511 was rebuilt in the baroque style.

Napoleon
When Napoleon established the Illyrian Provinces in 1809, in a bid to cut Habsburg Austria's access to the Adriatic, he made Ljubljana the capital; alas, Austrian rule was restored in 1813. The citizens, however, acquired a taste for independence.

Towards Independence
By the end of the 19th century, Ljubljana had become the centre of Slovenian nationalism under Austrian rule. Besides the obvious demand for political autonomy, Ljubljana was also a hotbed of cultural nationalism, best expressed by writers like France Prešeren (see p50) and Fran Levstik (1831–87), the first notable writer of Slovenian epic prose.

> **JASON AND THE DRAGON**
> Legend has it that on their return from their pilfering exploits, Jason and his fleece-stealing Argonauts camped along the banks of the Ljubljanica. Here they met a fearsome fire-breathing dragon. Being all man, Jason slayed the beast and went on his way, but this heroic episode was marked by the city fathers, who made the green dragon the symbol of Ljubljana.

Coats of arms in the Chapel of St George at Ljubljana Castle (p9)

The Two World Wars

Slovenia happily joined the Kingdom of Serbs, Croats and Slovenes after WWI. However, after the outbreak of WWII the city was occupied by the Italians and then the Germans, who cut the city off from the rest of the country, ringing it with barbed wire and turning it into a kind of ghetto.

Yugoslavia & Socialism

In 1945 Ljubljana became the capital of the Socialist Republic of Slovenia within Yugoslavia. For the next half-century or so it thrived as the most prosperous of Tito's six capitals, although many grumbled that the redistribution of Slovenia's wealth to less developed states was stifling Slovenian prosperity.

Independence

In 1991, Slovenia finally got what it always wanted: independence. Belgrade was willing to let the country go primarily because there wasn't a sizeable Serb minority within Slovenia. Since then the country has gone from strength to strength.

ENVIRONMENT

Ljubljana could easily be the poster-child for clean and healthy urban living. It's a small capital surrounded by lush countryside, low-lying hills and plenty of trees. But there is ample greenery within the city itself and the Ljubljančani have a highly developed sense of ecological and civic pride.

Just about everybody in Ljubljana recycles – most domestic refuse

DID YOU KNOW?
- Population: 269,824 (2001)
- Elevation: 298m
- Students: 58,000
- Number of theatres: 11
- Average temperature in January: 3.4°C
- Average temperature in July: 21.9°C

is disposed of neatly in bins that have three separate compartments – and almost everyone cycles. Neat, rust-red cycle paths are ubiquitous throughout the city.

GOVERNMENT & POLITICS

Slovenia's political history really took off in 1991 with the declaration of independence. It adopted a standard democratic model as its system of government, but the country holds regular referenda – easier with a small population – to monitor public opinion on such matters as weekend opening hours and membership of the EU and NATO (yes to both). The main players in the pre-independence, communist political landscape have had prominent roles in the new government (Dr Janez Drnvovsvek was prime minister and is now president) but in recent years the government has drifted to the right.

ECONOMY

A largely heterogeneous and highly adaptable economy has always been central to Ljubljana's prosperity, while Slovenia's accession to the EU in 2004 opened up a vast market for the country's goods.

The capital is responsible for around 25% of the country's GDP, primarily thanks to industry (pharmaceuticals, petrochemicals and food-processing), retailing, transport, communications and financial and other business services.

Tourism is increasingly important, with over 500,000 visitors a year and rising: when easyJet began flying directly into Ljubljana in 2004 it heralded an upward gear-shift in tourist numbers to the capital.

SOCIETY & CULTURE

And now for a little generalisation: Ljubljančani are a sophisticated, complex lot. Extremely well-educated, they have a reputation for being sober-minded, hard-working, dependable and honest – a Germanic bent that is the result of 600-plus years in the orbit of the Habsburgs. But they retain something of their Slavic character, even if their spontaneity is a little more planned and their expressions of passionate ardour a little more muted than that of their southern Slavic neighbours. Ljubljana – and Slovenia generally – has the best of two worlds: the stability of its Austro-German heritage and the fun-loving attitudes of its Slavic roots. A Germanic mind guiding a Slavic heart?

Ljubljana is a very urbane city, but its citizenry is passionately attached to the countryside. Like all Slovenes, Ljubljančani firmly believe that the essence of their national character lies in nature's plentiful bounty. For them a life that is not in some way connected

The Ljubljančani: a Slavic-Germanic mix

to the countryside is inconceivable. At weekends or at the end of a busy day's money-making many seek the great outdoors for a spot of hill-walking or cross-country skiing.

Although Ljubljana remains a largely liberal city – so long as you don't upset the status quo you can pretty much do as you please – there has of late been something of a right-wing backlash against anything to do with socialism or social liberalism. The current government is pretty right-wing, and it has made some awful comments in relation to homosexuality, race and other contentious issues. On the ground, however, Ljubljana thankfully remains quite accepting and pluralistic.

ARTS
Architecture

Ljubljana's dominant architectural styles – the Italian-influenced baroque of the 17th and 18th centuries and the Secessionist or art nouveau styles of the early 20th century – are the result of reconstruction following two devastating earthquakes, in 1511 and 1895. But no architect has had a greater impact on his city

The Urbanc building on Prešernov Trg (p8)

than Jože Plečnik (1872–1957); many of Ljubljana's most characteristic features, including Park Tivoli and Ljubljana's idiosyncratic recurring pyramid motifs, were his inspired design.

Literature

The dominant figure in Slovenian literature is the Romantic poet France Prešeren (1800–49), whose statue dominates Prešernov trg. Prešeren's patriotic yet humanistic verse was a driving force in raising Slovene national consciousness. Fittingly, a stanza of his poem *Zdravljica* (The Toast) is now the national anthem. The period from the turn of the 20th century up to WWII is dominated by two men who introduced modernism into Slovenian literature: the poet Oton Župančič (1878–1949) and the novelist and playwright Ivan Cankar (1876–1918). Contemporary writers and poets making use of avant-garde techniques include Drago Jančar (1948–), Tomaž Šalamun (1941–) and Kajetan Kovič (1931–).

Music

With four professional orchestras in such a small city, Ljubljana punches way above its musical weight. It has a long-established tradition of classical and modernist music – the country's best-known composer is Hugo Wolf (1860–1903) – but it was punk music in the late 1970s and early 1980s that put Ljubljana on the world stage with the emergence of art-punk group Laibach, who were imitated throughout Eastern Europe. The biggest band of the moment is Siddharta, who played to 30,000 people in Ljubljana in 2003 – over 10% of the city's population!

Directory

ARRIVAL & DEPARTURE
Air
Diminutive **Ljubljana Aerodrome** (code LJU; ☎ 04-206 19 81; www.lju-airport.si) is 23km north of the capital at Brnik, near Kranj. Six scheduled airlines serve more than 20 European destinations including Amsterdam, Dublin, Frankfurt, London, Manchester, Paris, Prague, Vienna and Zurich. Slovenia's national carrier, **Adria Airways** (airline code JP; ☎ 01-239 10 10; www.adria-airways.com), has regular direct flights to Prishtina, Podgorica, Skopje and Sarajevo.

INFORMATION
Car Park (first 30 min free, 1500SIT per day)
Ljubljanska Bank (☎ 04-206 16 79; ☯ 8am-3pm Mon-Fri)
Tourist Information Centre (☯ 11am-5.30pm Mon-Fri, to 4.30pm Sat)

AIRPORT ACCESS
Bus
City Bus (740SIT, 45-50 min) links the city centre with the airport from bus station lane 28. These run hourly, from 5.10am to 8.10pm Monday to Friday, but only seven times daily at weekends.

Another seven **Marun/Adria coaches** (1, E1; ☎ 04-252 10 16; 1000SIT, 30 min) run daily from the bust station.

The fancier hotels run an **airport shuttle** (2500SIT per person, 8800SIT per shuttle).

Taxi
A taxi to the city centre should cost about 7000SIT. There are always spanking white taxis waiting outside the arrivals terminal.

Bus
From the shed-like **bus station** (4, E1; ☎ 090 42 30, 090 42 40; www.ap-ljubljana.si; Trg Osvobodilne Fronte; ☯ 5.30am-9pm) buses run to destinations both within Slovenia and abroad. Next to the ticket windows are bilingual info-phones, and the timetable is very useful once you get the hang of it – nominate your destination first.

Car & Motorcycle
Ljubljana is at the centre of an extremely well-developed network of roads and motorways that link virtually every hamlet of a highly accessible country; you're never more than a couple of hours from an international border crossing and Slovenia has 150 of them, with Italy, Austria, Hungary and Croatia (although not all are open to citizens of third countries).

The major motorways serving Ljubljana are the A1, which runs diagonally across Slovenia from Leibnitz, in Austria to the northeast to Trieste, in Italy, to the southwest; the A2, which runs northwest past Bled to the Karavanke Tunnel and Austria; and the E70, which links Ljubljana with the Croatian border at Brežice.

Train
Domestic and international trains arrive at and depart from central Ljubljana's lone **train station** (4, F1; ☎ 291 33 32; Trg Osvobodilne, Fronte 6; ☯ 5am-10pm). Buy domestic tickets from windows 1 to 9 and international ones from No 10. You can get all the information you need from the **Info Center** (☯ 5.30am-9.30pm) in the main hall.

The lemon-yellow building houses a TIC branch office, bar, café, *okrepčevalnica* (snack bar), general store, McDonald's outlet and pizzeria.

Travel Documents
PASSPORT
As a rule a valid passport is all you need to enter the country for up to three months, even though EU, Croat and Swiss citizens need only flash their national ID cards on arrival for stays of up to 30 days. It's a good idea to carry your passport or other identification at all times.

VISA

Although Slovenia joined the EU in 2004, it is not scheduled to join the Schengen Zone until October 2007. Still, citizens of Australia, Canada, Israel, Japan, New Zealand, the USA and the EU do not require visas for stays of up to 90 days. South African passport-holders will require a visa.

Customs & Duty Free

Travellers can bring in the usual personal effects, clothes and electronic goods for their own use as well as 200 cigarettes (100 cigarillos, 50 cigars or 150g of tobacco), 2L of wine, 1L of spirits, 60ml of perfume and 250ml of eau de toilette. The import or export of more than 3,000,000SIT in cash without permission from the Bank of Slovenia is forbidden.

Slovenian customs inspections are rather cursory, but they do get sticky regarding pets: you'll need a rabies vaccination certificate (in English, German or Italian if you can't manage Slovenian) that is not less than 14 days or more than one year, and a vet's certificate of health no more than 10 days old.

Left Luggage

You can store bags at the **bus station** (4, E1; 320SIT; � 5am-8.30pm) and the **train station** (4, F1; 400SIT or €2; � 24hr). There are coin lockers on platform 1. Look for the '*garderoba*' signs.

GETTING AROUND

Ljubljana is a small, compact capital, which makes it a walker's dream. The heart of the city – Center and the Old Town – is easily managed on foot or by bike. Indeed, Ljubljana is a city of cyclists, and there are bike lanes and special traffic lights everywhere.

For destinations further afield or if you're staying out of town, the city has an efficient and user-friendly public transport system of 21 bus lines, run by **LPP** (Ljubljanski Potniški Promet; www.lpp.si, in Slovenian).

Throughout this book, we have used the 🚌 symbol followed by the relevant line number if that particular destination is best reached by bus rather than on foot; destinations within the city centre are eminently walkable to and from.

Travel Passes

You can buy a daily pass (*dnevna vozovnica*, 900SIT) or a weekly one (*tedenska vozovnica*, 3400SIT) from the **LPP Information Centre** (1, C2; ☎ 582 24 20; Slovenska cesta 55; � 6am-8pm Mon-Fri, 7am-8pm Sat, 9am-1pm & 2-8pm Sun). The best deal for the short-term visitor is with the Ljubljana Card (p9), which entitles the bearer to free travel for 72 hours as well as reductions to museums and other attractions.

Bus

Ljubljana has excellent city buses. There are a total of 21 lines (bizarrely, No 4 doesn't exist), and half a dozen of them (Nos 1, 2, 3, 6, 8 and 11) are considered main lines. Nos 2, 6 and 11 start at 3.15am and finish at midnight; the rest begin their runs at 5am and finish between 9pm and 10.30pm. Buses on the main lines run about every five to 15 minutes; the service is less frequent on other lines and on Sunday and holidays.

You can either pay the flat fare (300SIT) on board the bus with exact change or use a tiny plastic token (*žeton*, 190SIT) available at many newsstands, kiosks and post offices.

Taxi

Metered taxis can be hailed on the street or hired from ranks near the train station, at the TIC on Stritarjeva ulica, in front of the Hotel Slon on Slovenska cesta, or on Mestni trg. You can call a taxi on any one of 10 numbers: ☎ 9700 to ☎ 9709 inclusive. Flagfall is 190SIT, and the per-kilometre charge is 140 to 300SIT depending on the day of the week, whether you call ahead or hail a taxi on the street.

Car & Motorcycle

A compact city centre, an efficient public transport system and plenty of taxis makes bringing your own car to Ljubljana somewhat unnecessary and a potential headache. Parking is not easy in the centre and, if you're not prepared to pay in some form or another, you're bound to get a ticket, or even get towed away. Parking on the street costs from 100SIT an hour, but it can be difficult to find a space. There are car parks throughout the city, and their locations are indicated on most maps. They charge between 200 and 250SIT per hour.

PRACTICALITIES
Business Hours

The opening times (*delovni čas*) of shops, groceries and department stores, which are almost always posted on the door, are usually from about 8am to 7pm on weekdays and 8am until 1pm on Saturday – although some shops will remain open until 6pm. Sundays are still sacrosanct: although a handful of grocery stores, including some branches of the ubiquitous Mercator chain, open on Sunday most shopping areas are as lively as Chernobyl. Museums often close on Monday. Banks often take lengthy lunch breaks, although some also open Saturday mornings.

Restaurants typically open until at least 10pm, bars until midnight, though they may have longer hours on Friday and Saturday and shorter on Sunday.

The closer winter approaches the earlier many attractions close and the fewer visits they allow. This leads to intricately complex tables of opening times that are beyond the scope of this book to reproduce in detail. Fortunately, most attractions have websites and leaflets displaying complete schedules in their full glory.

Climate & When to Go

There is no bad time to visit Ljubljana. June to September is the peak season for tourists, when al fresco living is easy and temperatures oscillate between warm and pleasant and hot and humid. Conversely, lots of visitors means it's harder to get a room and restaurant tables are tough to get without a booking. Autumn is an ideal time to visit: still-warm days are coloured by falling leaves and the whole city has a gorgeous glow about it – not to mention the falling prices of hotel rooms. Winter is extremely cold, with snow making a regular appearance, but crisp, blue days are easily enjoyed if you're wrapped up – and the ski slopes are just a short drive away. December is festive time, with the whole city awash with decorations and mulled-wine-fuelled celebration (p41).

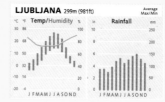

Disabled Travellers

Disabled facilities found throughout Ljubljana include public telephones with amplifiers, pedestrian crossings with beepers, occasionally lifts in pedestrian underpasses, sloped pavements and ramps in government buildings and reserved spaces in many car parks. An increasing number of hotels (mostly top-end, although not all) have rooms designed specially for disabled guests.

Discounts

Concessions (usually 20% to 50%) abound for youth, students and seniors on everything from transport to museums. (The minimum qualifying age for senior citizens is generally 60.) Bring whatever concession ID you have to flash. Holders of the Ljubljana Card (p9) get a plethora of discounts and concessions throughout the city.

Electricity
Voltage 220V
Frequency 50Hz
Cycle AC
Plugs two round pins

Embassies & Consulates
Slovenian representations abroad are fully listed on www.gov.si/mzz/eng and include:

Australia (☎ 02-624 34830; vca@mzz-dkp.gov.si; level 6, St George's Bldg, 60 Marcus Clarke St, Canberra ACT 2601)

Canada (☎ 613-565 5781; 150 Metcalfe St, Suite 2101, Ottawa)

Ireland (☎ 01-670 5240; Morrison Chambers, 32 Nassau St, Dublin)

New Zealand (☎ 04-567 0027; PO Box 30247, Eastern Hutt Rd, Pormare, Lower Hutt, Wellington)

UK (☎ 020-7222 5400; 10 Little College St, London SW1; ⏲ 9am-2pm Mon-Fri)

USA (☎ 202-667 5363; 1525 New Hampshire Ave NW, Washington DC)

Among the embassies and consulates in Ljubljana are:

Australia (4, B5; ☎ 425 42 52; Trg Republike 3/XII)

Canada (4, D2; ☎ 430 35 70; Miklošičeva cesta 19)

France (2, A1; ☎ 479 04 00; Barjanska cesta 1)

Germany (4, A4; ☎ 479 03 00; Prešernova cesta 27)

Ireland (4, E4; ☎ 300 89 70; Poljanski nasip 6)

Netherlands (4, E4; ☎ 420 14 61; Poljanski nasip 6)

New Zealand (3, off C1; ☎ 580 30 55; Verovškova 57)

South Africa (1, D2; ☎ 200 63 00; Pražakova 4)

UK (4, B5; ☎ 200 39 10; Trg Republike 3)

USA (4, A4; ☎ 200 55 00; Prešernova cesta 31)

Emergencies
In an emergency, the following numbers can be dialled:
Ambulance (Reševalci) ☎ 112
Automobile Assistance (AMZS) ☎ 19 87
Fire (Gasilci) ☎ 112
First Aid (Prva Pomoč) ☎ 112
Police (Policija) ☎ 113 (emergencies), 080 1200 (reporting crime etc)

Fitness
CYCLING
Ljubljana is a city of cyclists, and there are bike lanes and special traffic lights everywhere.

Ljubljana Bike (☎ 031-862 903; ⏲ 8am-8pm Jul-mid-Sep), run by the municipal government, offers visitors the free use of one-speed bicycles in summer from the train station, Prešernov trg and Trg Republike, just off Šubičeva ulica. You must produce ID and leave a 1000SIT deposit.

JOGGING & RUNNING
The vast expanse of Park Tivoli is the best spot for a long, uninterrupted run. You can run around the flat bits nearer the main entrances or really test your endurance up Rožnik Hill (p10).

SWIMMING & SAUNA
Tivoli Recreation Centre (4, A1; Rekreacijski Center Tivoli; ☎ 431 51 55; www.zavod-tivoli.si; Celovška cesta 25) in Park Tivoli has an indoor swimming pool (open September to May), a fitness centre, clay tennis courts and a roller-skating rink (which becomes an ice rink from mid-August to February). It also has a popular sauna called **Zlati Klub** (Gold Club; 4, A1; morning 2100SIT, afternoon 2400SIT; ⏲ 10am-8pm Mon, Wed, Thu & Sun men only, 10am-10pm Tue women only, 10am-midnight Fri & Sat mixed) with saunas, steam room, splash pools and outside swimming pool surrounded by high walls so you can sunbathe *au naturel*. Towels are an extra 500SIT.

Gay & Lesbian Travellers

Ljubljana is quietly conservative but deeply self-confident, remarkably broadminded and particularly tolerant. **Roza Klub** (4, C2; ☎ 01-430 47 40; Kersnikova ulica 4) is composed of gay and lesbian branches of the Student Cultural Centre (ŠKUC).

The **GALfon** (☎ 432 40 89; ⏰ 7-10pm) is a hotline and source of general information for gays and lesbians. The websites of **Slovenian Queer Resources Directory** (www.ljudmila.org/siqrd) and **Out In Slovenia** (www.outinslovenija. com) are both extensive and partially in English.

Health
MEDICAL SERVICES

EU citizens are covered for most medical care (except non-emergencies or emergency repatriation) with an EHIC card, obtainable through post offices in the UK. UK citizens also have the right to free medical care upon presentation of their passports. US citizens will have to ensure that they're covered for foreign travel with their own private health insurance companies.

Medical Centre (3, E3; Klinični Center; ☎ 522 50 50; Zaloška cesta 5-7; ⏰ 24hr) East of the Hotel Park in Tabor

Emergency Unit (3, E3; Urgenca; ☎ 232 30 60; Bohoričeva ulica 4; ⏰ 24hr) On the north side of the Medical Centre

DENTAL SERVICES

Dental Clinic (3, E3; Stomotološka Klinika; ☎ 431 31 13; Zaloška cesta 2; ⏰ 8am-noon Mon-Sat)

PHARMACIES

Central Pharmacy (4, D4; Centralna Lekarna; ☎ 230 62 00; Prešernov trg 5; ⏰ 7.30am-7.30pm Mon-Fri, 8am-1pm Sat)

Miklošič Pharmacy (4, D2; Lekarna Miklošič; ☎ 231 45 58; Miklošičeva cesta 24; ⏰ 24hr)

Holidays

1 & 2 January	New Year holidays
8 February	Prešeren Day (Slovenian Culture Day)
March-April	Easter Sunday & Monday
27 April	Insurrection Day
1 & 2 May	Labour Day holidays
25 June	National Day
15 August	Assumption Day
31 October	Reformation Day
1 November	All Saints' Day
25 December	Christmas Day
26 December	Independence Day

Internet

Virtually every hostel and hotel has some kind of Internet connection. You can also go online at:

Kotiček (4, E1; bus station; per 10min 100SIT; ⏰ 7am-8.30pm)

Napotnica.com (4, C3; Trg Ajdovščina 1; per 15min 200SIT; ⏰ 8am-11pm) Small café in the city centre mini-mall above the Pelican Pub.

Xplorer (4, D4; Petkovškovo nabrežje 23; per 5min 110SIT, per hr 800SIT; ⏰ 9am-11pm Mon-Fri, 1-11pm Sat & Sun) Good connection, plus discounts of 20% before noon, and 10% for students.

USEFUL WEBSITES

Ljubljana Calling (www.ljubljana-calling .com) Excellent, up-to-date listings.

Ljubljana Digital Media Lab (www. ljudmila.org) Links to all forms of alternative culture, music, venues and publications.

Ljubljana Life (http://geocities.com/ ljubljanalife) Website of the detailed listings freebie, including the *Slovenia Bulletin*, a weekly English-language review of the top stories in the Slovenian press.

Ljubljana Tourist Board (www.ljubljana-tourism.si) Your first portal of call for all things Ljubljanan.
University of Ljubljana (www.uni-lj.si) Useful info for students.

Lost Property

If you've lost something it may well turn up in the lost property room of the **Ljubljana-Centre Police Station** (4, D2; ☎ 432 03 41; www.policija.si; Trdinova ulica 10).

Metric System

The metric system is used in Slovenia and Slovenians use commas in decimals, and points to indicate thousands.

TEMPERATURE

°C = (°F - 32) ÷ 1.8
°F = (°C x 1.8) + 32

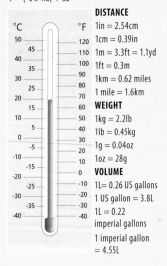

DISTANCE
1in = 2.54cm
1cm = 0.39in
1m = 3.3ft = 1.1yd
1ft = 0.3m
1km = 0.62 miles
1 mile = 1.6km
WEIGHT
1kg = 2.2lb
1lb = 0.45kg
1g = 0.04oz
1oz = 28g
VOLUME
1L= 0.26 US gallons
1 US gallon = 3.8L
1L = 0.22 imperial gallons
1 imperial gallon = 4.55L

Money
CHANGING MONEY

It is easy to change cash and travellers cheques at banks, post offices, tourist offices, travel agencies and private exchange offices. Look for the words *menjalnica* or *devizna blagajna* to guide you to the correct place or window.

CREDIT CARDS

Major credit and debit cards are accepted almost everywhere and ATMs are astonishingly ubiquitous.

If your credit card is lost, stolen or swallowed by an ATM, cancel the card immediately on these numbers in Ljubljana:

American Express	☎ 433 20 24
MasterCard	☎ 477 20 00
Visa	☎ 433 21 32

CURRENCY

Until 2007 Slovenia's legal currency will remain the tolar (SIT) but euros are already very widely accepted. Exchanging cash is simple at banks, major post offices, travel agencies and *menjalnica* (exchange bureaus).

EXCHANGE RATES

For current exchange rates see www.xe.com.

Australia	A$1	148SIT
Canada	C$1	176SIT
Croatia	1HRK	33SIT
Euro zone	€1	239SIT
Japan	¥100	170SIT
New Zealand	NZ$1	130SIT
UK	£1	349SIT
USA	US$1	201SIT

TRAVELLERS CHEQUES

Banks often give a better rate for travellers cheques than for cash, but some private exchange offices (not travel agencies) and post offices (if they accept them at all) do the opposite.

Newspapers & Magazines

Many British and American newspapers are available on the day of publication (late afternoon) at kiosks, hotels and bookshops in Ljubljana. The following English-language publications are available in Ljubljana:
Slovenia Times (www.sloveniatimes.com), an independent free newspaper that comes out every three weeks or so

Slovenija (www.zdruzenje-sim.si), a glossy quarterly with a heavy focus on culture *Ljubljana Life* (http://geocities.com/ljubljana-nalife), an excellent free bimonthly magazine that carries useful listings of restaurants, bars and other nightlife in the capital.

Post

Post office (4, C4; Slovenska cesta 32; ☯ 7am-8pm Mon-Fri, 7am-1pm Sat) Poste restante *(poštno ležeče)* held here for 30 days.

Post office branch (4, D1; Trg OF 5; ☯ 7am-midnight Mon-Fri, 7am-6pm Sat, 9am-noon Sun) Due west of the train station.

POSTAL RATES

Stamps *(znamke)* are sold at post offices and at some newsstands. A domestic/international letter *(pisma)* up to 100g costs 57/107SIT. There's a uniform rate of 83SIT for postcards.

Radio

Radio Slovenija 1 (88.5, 90.0, 90.9, 91.8, 92.0, 92.9, 94.1, 96.4 MHz FM & 918 kHz AM) has a nightly news bulletin broadcast in English at 10.30pm.

Telephone

Public telephones require a phonecard *(telefonska kartica)*. These are available at post offices and most newsstands. The cheapest phonecard (700SIT, 25-unit) gives about four minutes' calling time to other European countries. Most Ljubljančani have a mobile phone these days and indeed, some businesses quote only a mobile number. Mobile numbers are identifiable by codes 030, 031, 040 and 041.

Time

Slovenia lies in the Central European time zone. Winter time is GMT plus one hour and in summer it's GMT plus two hours. Clocks are put forward one hour at 2am on the last Sunday in March and turned back at the same time on the last Sunday in October.

Tipping

Although most Ljubljančani don't bother tipping more than a few coins – a hangover of the old regime – a tipping culture is growing, thanks in part to foreign visitors: 10% for standard service, up to 15% for better. It's entirely up to you.

Toilets

There are free public toilets in the train station and pay toilets (40SIT) below Triple Bridge in Prešernov trg – the latter are the cleanest public toilets we've ever seen. Generally there's no problem ducking into a restaurant to use the services.

Tourist Information

All three TICs have great free maps, themed brochures, tips and events listings. A new service handles ticketing for all the city's cultural events, including festivals, concerts, sporting events and fairs.

City Museum Cultural & Information Centre (4, B6; ☎ 251 40 25; www.mm-lj.si; Trg Francoske Revolucije 7; ☯ 10am-6pm Mon-Fri, 10am-1pm Sat) Information on museums, galleries and exhibitions in Ljubljana.

Ljubljana Tourist Information Centre (TIC; 4, D5; www.ljubljana-tourism.si; Stritarjeva 2; ☎ 306 12 15; ☯ 8am-9pm Jun-Sep, to 7pm Oct-May)

TIC Train Station (4, F1; ☎ 433 94 75; ☯ 8am-10pm Jun-Sep, to 7pm Oct-May)

Slovenian Tourist Information Centre (STIC; 4, E4; ☎ 306 45 75; www.slovenia-tourism.si; Krekov trg 10; ☯ 8am-9pm Jun-Sep, to 7pm Oct-May) Internet and bicycle hire available. Also, a free basic course in Slovenian is offered each Wednesday from 5pm to 6.30pm.

Women Travellers

Travelling as a single woman in Slovenia is little different from travelling in most Western European countries. If you can handle yourself in the occasional less-than-comfortable situation, you'll be fine.

LANGUAGE

Slovene is the official language of the Republic of Slovenia and it's what you'll hear in Ljubljana but virtually everyone in Slovenia speaks at least one other language. However, the fact that you'll rarely have difficulty making yourself understood and that you'll probably never 'need' Slovene shouldn't stop you from learning a few words and phrases from this rich and wonderful language.

PRONUNCIATION

No sounds in Slovene are difficult for a speaker of English to learn.

VOWELS

a   as the 'u' in 'cut'
e   as the 'a' in 'hat'; as the 'e' in 'they'; when unstressed, as the 'a' in 'ago'
i   short, as in 'ink'; long as in 'marine'
o   as in 'off'; also as in 'or'
u   as in 'put'

CONSONANTS

c   as the 'ts' in 'cats'
č   as the 'ch' in 'chip'
g   as in 'gold'
j   as the 'y' in 'yellow'
r   a rolled 'r'
š   as the 'sh' in 'ship'
ž   as the 's' in 'pleasure'

BASICS

Good day/Hello.	Dober dan.
Hi.	Pozdravljeni/ Pozdravljen. (polite/informal)
Goodbye.	Nasvidenje.
Please.	Prosim.
Thank you.	Hvala.
Yes.	Da/Ja.
No.	Ne.
Excuse me.	Dovolite mi, prosim.
Sorry.	Oprostite/Oprosti. (pol/inf)
My name is ...	Jaz sem ...
I'm from ...	Sem iz ...

ACCOMMODATION

I'm looking for	Iščem ...
a guesthouse	gostišče
a hotel	hotel
I'd like a ...	Rad/Rada bi ... (m/f)
Do you have a ...?	Ali imate prosto ...?
single room	enoposteljno sobo
double room	dvoposteljno sobo
room with a	sobo z
bathroom	kopalnico
How much is it ...?	Koliko stane ...?
per night	na noč
per person	po osebi
May I see the room?	Lahko vidim sobo?
I'm/We're leaving today.	Danes odhajam/ odhajamo.

DIRECTIONS

Where is ...?	Kje je ...?
How do I get to ...?	Kako pridem do ...?
Is it near/far?	Ali je blizu/daleč?
(Go) straight ahead.	(Pojdite) naravnost naprej.
(Turn) left/right at ...	(Obrnite) levo/desno pri ...
the corner	vogalu
the traffic lights	semaforju

EMERGENCIES

Help!	Napomoč!
There's been an accident!	Nesreča se je zgodila!
Call ...!	Pokličite ...!
a doctor	zdravnika
the police	policijo
I'm lost.	Izgubil/zgubila sem se. (m/f)
I'm sick.	Bolan/Bolna sem. (m/f)
Could you please help me?	Mi lahko pomagate?
Go away!	Pojditestran!

LANGUAGE DIFFICULTIES

Do you speak English?	Govorite angleško?
I understand.	Razumem.
I (don't) understand.	(Ne) razumem.
Could you repeat that, please?	Lahko ponovite?
Could you write it down, please?	Lahko to napišete?
Can you show me (on the map)?	A mi lahko pokažete (na mapi)?
What does ... mean?	Kaj ... pomeni?

NUMBERS

1	ena
2	dve
3	tri
4	štiri
5	pet
6	šest
7	sedem
8	osem
9	devet
10	deset
100	sto
1000	tisoč

SHOPPING & SERVICES

I'd like to buy ...	Rad bi kupil/kupila ...
I'm just looking.	Samo gledam.
How much is it?	Koliko stane?
I don't like it.	Ni mi všeč.
It's too expensive for me.	Predrago je zame.
It's cheap.	Poceni je.
May I look at it?	Ali lahko pogledam?
I'll take it.	Kupil/Kupila bom. (m/f)
I'm looking for a/the	Iščem ...
Where is a/the ...?	Kje je ...?
bank	banka
chemist	lekarna
city centre	središče mesta
exchange office	menjalnica
hospital	bolnica
market	tržnica
police	policija

post office	pošta
public phone	javni telefon
public toilet	javno stranišče
tourist office	turistični urad
What time does it open/close?	Kdaj se odpre/ zapre?
I'd like to change some ...	Rad bi zamenjal nekaj ...
money	denarja
travellers cheques	potovalnih čekov
Do you accept credit cards?	Ali vzamete kreditne karte?

TIME & DATES

What time is it?	Koliko je ura?
It's ...	Ura je ...
(eight) o'clock	osem
(one) o'clock	end
seven thirty	pol osem
a quarter to	četrt do
a quarter past	in četrt
in the morning	zjutraj
in the evening	zvečer
today	danes
tonight	nocoj
tomorrow	jutri
yesterday	včeraj
Monday	ponedeljek
Tuesday	torek
Wednesday	sreda
Thursday	četrtek
Friday	petek
Saturday	sobota
Sunday	nedelja

TRANSPORT

What time does the ... leave?	Kdaj odpelje ...?
boat/ferry	ladja/trajekt
bus	avtobus
plane	avion
train	vlak
I want to go to ...	Želim iti ...

Index

See also separate indexes for Eating (p62), Sleeping (p62), Shopping (p62) and Sights with map references (p62).

FEATURES

Pri Sv Florijanu	*Eating*
Jazz Club Gajo	*Entertainment*
Bar Minimal	*Drinking*
Café Antico	*Café*
Ljubljana Castle	*Highlights*
Maximarket	*Shopping*
City Museum	*Sights/Activities*
Hotel Lev	*Sleeping*
Bled	*Trips & Tours*

AREAS

	Beach, Desert
	Building
	Land
	Mall
	Market
	Other Area
	Park/Cemetery
	Sports
	Urban

HYDROGRAPHY

	River, Creek
	Water

BOUNDARIES

	International
	State, Provincial
	Regional, Suburb
	Ancient Wall

ROUTES

	Tollway
	Freeway
	Primary Road
	Secondary Road
	Tertiary Road
	Lane
	Under Construction
	One-Way Street
	Unsealed Road
	Mall/Steps
	Tunnel
	Walking Path
	Walking Trail/Track
	Pedestrian Overpass
	Walking Tour

TRANSPORT

	Airport, Airfield
	Bus Route
	Cable-Car, Funicular
	Cycling, Bicycle Path
	Ferry
	General Transport
	Metro
	Rail
	Taxi Rank
	Tram

SYMBOLS

	Bank, ATM
	Beach
	Buddhist
	Castle, Fortress
	Christian
	Embassy, Consulate
	Hospital, Clinic
	Information
	Internet Access
	Islamic
	Jewish
	Lighthouse
	Lookout
	Monument
	Mountain, Volcano
	National Park
	Parking Area
	Petrol Station
	Picnic Area
	Point of Interest
	Police Station
	Post Office
	Ruin
	Telephone
	Toilets
	Zoo, Bird Sanctuary
	Waterfall

24/7 travel advice
www.lonelyplanet.com